AROUND SEATTLE IN 80 DATES – AN ONLINE DATING JOURNEY

RENATA M. LUBINSKY

Around Seattle in 80 Dates -- An Online Dating Journey
Copyright ©2018 by Renata M. Lubinsky
All rights reserved.

Cover Design: Ada Frost, http://adafrost.co.uk/

Editing and formatting: Patricia Zick, The Manuscript Doctor, http://www.pczickeditor.wordpress.com/

Cover photography: Dana Photography, https://www.facebook.com/DanaBPhotograph/

This book contains stories that express the opinion of the author and are written to express one person's point of view and not to infringe on anyone else's right. No part of this book may be used or reproduced in any manner without written permission from the author, except in the case of brief quotations embodied in critical articles or reviews.

Contact: Renata M. Lubinsky at renata.lubinsky1@gmail.com

ISBN-13: **978-1985371873**
ISBN-10: **1985371871**

DEDICATION

To my daughters, my baby sister, and amazing girlfriends - for all your patience and support. I love you from here to Israel.

To my one and only Mike, who believed in me and joined the ride with no hesitations. You are a real *Mensch*. I could have not done it without you.

To the Internet for online dating and the endless options it brought with it.

TABLE OF CONTENTS

DEDICATION iii
TABLE OF CONTENTS v
1 - AROUND SEATTLE IN 80 DATES – Where It All Started 1
2 - LET'S GET OUT OF HERE 5
3 - A COUGAR IN GOA 27
4 - ONCE I TRIED GOING BLACK 44
5 - HOW THICK IS YOUR DICK? 99
6 - YOUNG DOLLY PARTON 102
7 - SIXTY-NINE IS NOT ALWAYS A GOOD NUMBER 116
8 - MY OWN POPEYE 123
9 - I MOVED TO A GRAVEYARD 137
10 - NO PLACE LIKE HOME 144
11 - MIKE MOTEK 185
12 - DOUBLE DIPPING 198
13 - MIKE #77 238
14 - #80 FOREVER 244
15 - TO DO OR NOT TO DO – ONLINE DATING 266
THANK YOU 278
RESOURCES 279
ABOUT THE AUTHOR 280

1 - AROUND SEATTLE IN 80 DATES – WHERE IT ALL STARTED

I started dating men when I turned forty-seven. Until then, I had been with the same man for thirty-two years. We met when I was only fourteen, and I married him twice—once when I turned twenty after my mandatory military IDF (Israeli Defense Forces) service in Israel, and then again, when I was twenty-four. But that is a different story.

I was devastated when my marriage ended. I called the only woman with whom I had any personal connection, a coworker, and cried for hours, thinking that my sex life was over. Who on earth would want to date me, let alone go down on me at my age? Forget about it.

I'm a natural blonde with long hair and blue eyes. I'm 5' 2"—when I stretch—and I'm very curvy. In fact, my nickname on my favorite dating site was "Young Dolly Parton."

But at forty-seven, I was no Dolly. In fact, I felt more like I had hit a dead end—a single mother in a foreign country with no family support, no friends or girlfriends, and two kids. And as for men, I was sure that door had closed.

But I didn't stay down for long. I picked myself up, dusted the self-pity off my shoulders, and joined a few dating sites. It took exactly two hours for my first suitor to reach out, and then there was a second, a third, and then dozens more. I was bombarded by men asking to meet me and get to know me. Some were quite clear about what they meant by "getting to know me," and they were weeded out very quickly. My pictures were clear, and I posted non-body pics—only my smiling face—but I still got their attention.

I can say with certainty that going on these dates was the best cure in the world for the rebound blues. As I started going out more frequently on dates, I felt surer of myself and more confident. Every new message on the online dating site was a promise for fun, a fantastic time, and a unique experience. A long-term relationship was not something I even considered at that point. I was still healing and needed to take care of myself first. Settling down was not in my "wish list."

Soon after I started dating, I found myself driving around Issaquah, a lovely town snuggled near the mountains outside of Seattle where I lived. The local theater was playing the classic, *Around the World in 80 Days*. An epiphany! This was precisely what I was going to do—a twist on the theme. I would experience Seattle in eighty dates. I loved touring the city, visiting the local bars, learning about the area, you name it. What could be better than doing that while going out with a new guy to a new place on each occasion? Perfect! A win-win situation for all involved.

And so, it began. I found most of my dates online. Strangely, sixty percent of the men I dated/met/chatted with were named Mike. So, to make things easier, all the men in my stories are called Mike, with either a number, corresponding to where they were in my "eighty dates" list, or I assigned them a nickname. I notified the significant Mikes about my project, and all were on board and supportive.

To reach my goal, I had to get busy. Some days I scheduled myself for as many as five separate dates! How did I manage this? Elementary plan: breakfast, lunch, happy hour, dinner, and a late-night glass of wine. The whole project took a year and a half.

Before I begin recounting this journey, I want to say thank you to my very new but close girlfriends who listened to me in the wee hours without judging and with no small amount of wine. I could not have done it without them. I'm also thankful for my younger sister, who lives in Israel—while I live in Seattle. She heard all these stories, and even "joined" me sometimes on my dates through phone chats. She's not only my sister, but she is also my best friend and an amazing one.

And, a huge shout-out to my two lovely daughters. They saw me cry, laugh, fall in love, and go out on dates again and again. They also came to support me on stage—I'm a stand-up comedienne and a storyteller in the Seattle area— despite being thoroughly embarrassed. I will always be their mom, and no doubt the cause of their weekly therapy sessions.

2 - LET'S GET OUT OF HERE

The separation talk with the husband was terrible, awful. After thirty-two years together, it is not easy for the mind and body to say goodbye and end a marriage to a man I met when I was just a kid. A man with whom I imagined spending my whole life and with whom I share two kids. But life goes on, and after the talk, I decided it was time to get back out there and start a new chapter of my life. I needed to check my market value.

I was fourteen and a half when I met my future husband. I married him when I turned twenty, after service in the IDF. I was forty-seven and the mother of two girls when we had the talk. We lived on the other side of the world from our home in Israel, far from all our family and friends. I felt alone, but I knew myself, and I knew things would change if I did something to turn them. This was how I usually felt in my life, but for some reason, I did not feel so sure right then. I was in Seattle, and I felt alone.

I could not imagine another man ever wanting me. A man who needed me desperately, for my body and my mind. And a man who'd go down on me? Oh no, this would never happen again, right? Forty-seven years old, 5' 2", blonde, and oh yes, with some curves that I completely forgot about for years while I was busy with working, raising kids, and living life. The story is the same for so many women who give their all to their families and work, I guess. But at that point, I declared, "It is all about me," and I was sure I was the only one in the world who ever felt that way.

When I shared my concerns with my girlfriend, Maxine, I was in tears. She was my only girlfriend in Seattle at that time. Maxine was a gorgeous woman, 6' 2", and married for the third time to a handsome black man who was 6' 5". She's white, and she likes only black guys. I cried to her that I was quite sure the end of my world had arrived, and my sex life was over. Yes, sex was essential to me, especially at that time when I felt so vulnerable. Good sex always made me thrive.

Maxine started to laugh hysterically. I was confused. What was going on?

"Maxine, I'm serious, nobody will ever want to date me. My sex life is over!"

Maxine was usually very professional and politically correct. But it was different when we had a "girlfriend talk." It took few minutes until Maxine stopped laughing and was able to speak again.

"Honey," she said, "go look in the mirror. Don't even worry and relax, you will have a line of men knocking on your door."

She doesn't understand, I thought at the time. She has never been in my shoes.

I had a lot of weird and not so smart thoughts during those first days, including the idea of joining a monastery, but I'm Jewish so that wouldn't work. Sometimes I made myself smile with my crazy ideas, and I saw them for what they could be— a good start to stop feeling sorry for myself and an opportunity for some good stand-up material that could be used on stage. You get lemons, you make Limoncello, right? I always had a good bottle of vodka in the cabinet.

Three weeks of daily crying was enough. It was time to start a new journey, and I was going to discover "my value" in the singles' world.

It was a Friday night, and I was on my way out to visit a wine bar with my new girlfriend, Tina. We were about to join a "meetup" group that she had joined and whose members shared a mutual interest in wine tasting. The wine bar was located in our neighborhood, and I had visited there before. We both liked the place, and Tina made sure I was in a good mood, chatting with me and telling me funny stories from her life. Since Tina was a new girlfriend, we were just getting to know each other. It was one of those falling in love moments that you have in life—if you are lucky—with people. We met, and we fell in love on the spot. As girlfriends, that is.

When we walked in the bar, we immediately identified the meetup group by a small sign on their table. *Oh no, I'm not sitting there*, I thought. What I saw at that moment, was a group of older people who all looked grumpy. Exactly what I didn't need right then.

"I'm going to the restroom," I blurted out and then I darted toward the ladies' room. There was a line (surprise, surprise), and I happily and patiently waited my turn; knowing what awaited me back at the table.

Situated in downtown Issaquah, this fun and friendly wine bar occupies a small space, and most of the people in the place greet each other by their first name.

I had visited the place a few times and enjoyed it. A few weeks before, following a small talk I had with the owner while I sat at the bar, I found out that the owner is Jewish. When I confessed that I was Jewish as well and my accent came from Israel—nobody is perfect besides Wonder Women, Gal Gadot, and even she has an Israeli accent—I was adopted on the spot and became part of the family. Since then, every time I visited the place, I was identified as a relative, receiving hugs and kisses from the owner and his sister who ran the bar. The owner's son, a very hip young man in his early twenties, always made sure to stop everything and step over to kiss and greet me and my date(s) when I arrived. Never had a "home bar," and this one ultimately felt like one.

The owner, who knew most of the crowd, greeted everybody with a smile; a handshake with the men and a peck on the cheek for the ladies in the group. His warm welcome makes customers want to go back and visit the place often.

The line to the only ladies' bathroom was taking a while, which provided me the time to look around and see what was going on that night. To my left, there was a fireplace with a couple of single-seat couches, and in one of them sat a handsome guy, in his early forties, with a single glass of wine. The seat next to him was free, and there was no glass on the table beside it. It is all about details, right?

We examined each other. Briefly, our eyes connected for a few crucial seconds, flirting, and then started all over again. I could feel the stranger's eyes on me while he examined my face, scanned my body, from bottom to top. My turn to enter the bathroom arrived, and unfortunately, I had to move from my spot.

Once out of the bathroom, I walked toward the guy, approached him, and leaned over his right shoulder. I could smell his gentle but firm aftershave, while I whispered in his ear, "Is this seat taken?"

"No," he said right away, and straightened up in his chair.

"Oh, okay. Just wanted to know." I smiled as I headed back to the "meetup" table.

He stopped me by grabbing my hand. "You are welcome to join me."

"Thank you, I will. I just need to let my girlfriend know where I am," I replied, thoroughly pleased with myself.

Oh boy, was I happy with myself? This was the handsomest man in the room. He was dressed in nice jeans and a black button-down shirt with an Asian pattern. Exactly my style. He had a goatee beard (*hmm.... I wonder how it feels*), and I think I saw a tattoo on his chest when I bent to whisper in his ear. And, he was apparently very fit.

The walk back to the "meetup" table was no more than thirty steps, but the place was so crowded that I had to stop and let the traffic jam clear. I also had a chance to say hi to the owner who was tending bar that night. He shouted out a "Shalom" and winked at me. *Ahhhh...A feeling of home...what a small Shalom can do.*

When I got back to the table, I noticed that the place was now completely full, and more people had joined the table. My girlfriend, Tina, was in the middle of a lively discussion with the people around the table.

"Tina," I said, "I'm going to join this guy in the back."

"What?" she cried. "What happened? You were gone for five minutes, and you already met somebody?"

I smiled and nodded my head. "Can I buy you a drink?"

I tried to be super sweet, as I was about to ditch her. I never ditched a friend like that before. I was doing everything I could to kiss Tina's ass.

I got us both a drink, we clinked glasses, she in her native Dutch—*Proost*—and me in Hebrew—*Le'Hayim*; and then she smiled at me. I knew she understood.

"Don't do anything stupid," she said.

"I promise," I told her. What I was really thinking was that stupid is a vast range and can be understood differently by different people, and off I went.

I wore a short black mini-skirt, black lace pantyhose, and a half-see-through blouse. I was sober, and I felt hot. The song "I'm too sexy for my shirt" played in my mind. It was Nineties' Night, and the cover band was excellent. The dance floor was small, and a bunch of people were already dancing and filling it. I loved this kind of music, and I loved to dance.

I finally wound my way through the crowd and got back to my black knight. Well, black clothes. He looked and sounded very white. I glided into the single couch next to him. I noticed that he had a fresh new glass of wine. "Anything for you?" he asked.

"No thanks, just got myself a glass," and I showed him my wine. We introduced ourselves by names. First name only, and his was Mike—he would become Mike #1. I'm always having fun when I introduce myself for the first time. My name is different, my accent is different, and it usually takes three times until the other person gets it right. I sometimes even need to spell it out slowly and only then does the other person get it. R like Robert, and I start with a rolling "RRRR" sound.

Mike #1 surprised me and got my name right the first time I said it despite the noise level in the crowded room. I soon learned that Mike #1 was visiting the place alone. He came to see the band that was playing that night. Yes, he too loved to dance. And his hand was suddenly on my knee, softly patting my lace pantyhose. I felt as if my heart would stop beating any minute, my face turned red, and then I felt the hot flashes…

Is it the "normal" hot flashes I'm having thanks to my age, or is it something else?

I thought it was something else, and I smiled to myself. It felt like a different very intense hot flash. Ouch.

Mike #1 saw me smiling and grabbed my hand. He pulled me toward the dance floor. Not only was Mike #1 attractive while seated, but he was also very handsome when he stood up, and he smelled fantastic. I could not stop looking at him. Mike #1 kept one of his hands on me all the time, even while we danced and moved around.

Mike #1 was only a bit taller than me. I was wearing very short heels that day. I usually look for tall guys, but then Mike #1 was the best I could ask for. He was just perfect.

Mike #1's touch was soft but also firm. There was not a second that he was not touching me. Softly, but definitely, he made sure to let me know he was there connecting with me. He was very much the man. This was a very new feeling to me.

We danced to a couple of songs and returned to our seats. I sipped my wine slowly and felt Mike #1's hand briefly touching my arm. And then Mike #1 began to pet my arm softly. The place was darkish, and it felt as if we were alone and could do whatever we wanted.

We exchanged necessary information, such as the origin of my accent—first question always—followed by asking what I was doing in Seattle. I usually said, "Long story. Let's just say I live in the area and work as a project manager." Ninety-nine percent of the people in Seattle know what that means. Mike #1 was a Quality Assurance engineer. We both worked in the same field — software, the geek's world. If what was going on was geeky, please bring it on. I never thought that a geek could look so good, dress up so nicely, and touch like that.

And then his hand moved to my knee. He told me he really liked the lace.

"Let's get out of here." Mike #1 turned around to me and said it softly and firmly at the same time.

I froze. This was the point I was sure I was part of a movie scene, and I was dreaming. I've never been to an adult movie, but now it felt as if I was becoming the star of one. My wine glass was still full. I didn't have a chance to touch it, and now I couldn't reach it. I felt as if I was floating, and I was dizzy with excitement. I needed to think fast.

"Okay," I said, "but wait, my girlfriend is here. I need to let her know I'm going." Then I added, "If you want me in your car I need you to show me your ID and send me a photo of it." I don't know where this Polish/Jewish responsibility came from in the middle of the sexiest moment of my life. I had just asked Mike #1, the most exciting man in the room, to send me a copy of his driver's license so I could send it to my girlfriend.

The joy of being a woman in this world.

Mike #1 was not confused, nor did he hesitate a second. He took out his wallet and pulled out his license. I took a picture with my phone, kissed him on the cheek, and started to send the photo to Tina.

"I'll be right back," I said to Mike #1 and went on my way to where Tina and the meetup group were seated. It was going to be an amazing night. I felt it everywhere in my body. The band just started to play, "I got a feeling that tonight's going to be a good night," and boy, did I agree. What a coincidence that this song played, but who am I to argue? I managed to finally send the picture to Tina, while still being stuck in the middle of the crowd, trying to get back to where I left her.

When I reached Tina, she looked baffled. "What is going on?" she asked me. "I just got a pic of a driver's license of some guy from you?"

I started laughing, "And yes, I'm leaving with him right now. Come and meet him. He's really cool."

Tina and I had met about a month earlier in a women's meetup (yes, I know…these meetups are all over the place,) and we fell in love immediately. It was a Halloween party, and we clicked right away. Tina is Dutch, speaks six languages and has traveled the world, including Asia, which she loved. My house was in the boonies. My closest neighbors were few minutes' walk away, with a forest between us. We discovered immediately that Tina lived just two miles away, in the same neighborhood. "How crazy was this," we both said when we first met. And then we started visiting each other. Tina has a nine-year-old son and is married to a successful sales manager. Tina has not worked since she became a mom. Their home is beautiful, and Tina is very much into arts and crafts, gardening, and wine, which means we have a lot in common. We love drinking wine together, going out with other ladies and talking for hours about our trips, living in Europe versus the USA, and food. Tina specializes in oriental cuisine, and I love it as well. We kept discovering common interests that we both enjoyed. Tina loved dancing, was a fun woman, and we were in the process of building a strong friendship. Although we had not known each other for a long time, we already had some interesting very open discussions, which brought us closer.

Tina followed me back to the table where I had left Mike #1. This meant another pass through a crowded room that made me feel like a salmon swimming upstream. It was more crowded than it was ten minutes earlier, and we had to push our way to get there. We finally made our way, and I introduced them to each other. Tina gave me a hug and a kiss with a big smile and shining eyes. "Have fun," she said, and Mike #1 and I left the place and headed for his car. I had ridden with Tina, so it was a relief that I didn't have a car to consider.

We stopped at a nearby grocery store, which was open until midnight. It was still early in the evening, and it had just started to get dark. Mike #1 bought some protection.

"Three? You need three of them?" I asked him with a smile.

He did not answer me, but he smiled back. He also bought a bottle of wine. I decided to buy flowers to bring with us to the room. *To make it more personal.* Flowers make everything always look better.

Our next stop was the motel next to the IHOP, exit 15 off I-90. I waited in the car, a big comfortable BMW with dark windows. I closed my eyes and started breathing exercises. Two hundred crazy thoughts ran through my head, so I tried to meditate; to relax. Suddenly, my phone rang. It was my baby sister from the other side of the world. We are best friends, besides her being my baby sister, and we have daily calls while she is on her way to work, in an opposite time zone in Israel. There was a seven-year difference between us, but it had no meaning at our respective ages. I share everything with her.

"Where are you?" she asked.

"I don't think you want to know." I giggled but tried to stop myself and sound serious, but I just couldn't.

My baby sister insisted. "Yes, I do, where are you, my crazy sis, and what are you up to?"

I told her the whole story, in ten succinct sentences, and then I heard silence on the other side.

"OMG, Sis, you are crazy," she finally said.

"I know," I answered, "and I love it." We finished the call just as Mike #1 returned to the car. I shared with him that I was just on the phone with my baby sister from Israel. He smiled and just held my hand and kissed it. At that point, I completely melted into my seat, and I kissed his hand back.

We entered the room. Mike #1 opened the wine, and I made sure the flowers were centered on the table. He loved the flowers, and I received another kiss on my hand. Mike #1 also bought a candle and lit it. This was also the moment when I turned my back to him to take off my shoes.

Six hours later, we fell asleep. I woke up at four in the morning, with a huge smile and a lovely tickling feeling between my legs. I was ready for more, but I needed to get back home. My daughter, sixteen years old, was there alone, and I hadn't told her I wasn't coming home that night, as I hadn't planned the evening to go the way it had, of course. And then I remembered., I didn't have my car.

Tina had driven the night before, and I left her there — okay, I kind of ditched her, really. I made a mental note to take care of this later.

Mike #1 woke up as well and started touching me in all the best places from the night before. OMG, what had I been afraid of? Nobody would want to go down on me, and I wouldn't have sex anymore? Where did I get that stupid idea? I had just discovered a new world of pleasure that I had been missing all those years. What had I been thinking? Blonde, blonde, blonde.

We took our time, and then it was 5:30 a.m., and I really had to get to my place before my daughter woke up. Mike #1 took me home, a fifteen-minute drive from the motel.

My house was in the middle of a forest, and I saw Mike #1's eyes open wide when we got to my place. The area where I lived was beautiful and picturesque. The house sat on an acre of land, with deer and bunnies running around the property, and bears crossing the yard in the summertime. The area was well maintained and had a private road leading to the house. I'd been working hard every day to garden the large yard, as my about-to-be ex-husband had left the house a few weeks earlier, and all the work was now done by me. Mike #1 was impressed, and I smiled to myself. If only he knew how stressed I was every month to pay the mortgage and the bills while maintaining the place. The house would have to be sold very soon.

Mike #1 dropped me at home, and we said goodbye with a long sensational kiss. Mike #1 stopped me at one point and gave me a soft kiss on my forehead. I love kisses on my forehead. They relax me, and I feel no wrinkles for few minutes. It feels like all my worries are taken away. Peaceful feeling. He drove away, and I sighed. It had been a big milestone night for me. I just did what I saw in the movies and read about in books for years. I walked into a bar and left with a guy for the night. And it was the first time I had left my house since my divorce and mingled with men as a single woman. *The MOJO was there*. I was very proud of myself. Life had not ended along with my marriage.

I saw Mike #1 the next day, and we had another hot round, but I couldn't tell you where it was.

Two days later, I left for four weeks on a business trip and traveled to India and Israel. We also said goodbye before I left, and I updated Mike #1 with the date of my return. He called me a day after I landed, and we took it from there.

Mike #1 and I kept in touch for the next year, with weird text messages from his side— boobies massage clip versus a thirty-minute video clip about a rabbi who sexually abused a boy in a Yeshiva. I texted Mike #1 one morning at seven and asked him if he was busy. He was at home working out on his treadmill. I asked if he wanted to continue his exercise in my bedroom. His answer was "Yes," and he was at my place in thirty minutes where we continued the morning with some hard-core moves. I loved his body, and I loved his hands on me. He surprised me every time with new moves and ideas that made me cry for help while at the same time asking him not to stop. It all was unique and fascinating to me.

At one point, and after different sexy texts and video clips that we were sending to each other, Mike #1 offered to take me to a swingers' club. I was dying to see a place like that, as it came up in multiple discussions in various locations and with different people. I agreed, on one condition. Tina would join us. Tina wanted to see this kind of place as well.

Tina got married when she was nineteen, and at the time, she was forty-four. She never had these kinds of experiences. For both of us, it was like going to a museum, visiting an exhibition and seeing a new and different costume—something both Tina and I loved to do and did all over the world. It was like looking into another culture, or subculture maybe? Who are these people and how does it work? I said yes to the offer, and Mike #1 agreed to my one condition.

He arranged for a guy friend of his to join us, as women could bring a guy with them, but a guy couldn't just walk in without a female companion. Even though a guy had to be accompanied by a woman, a woman could step in by herself. Not sure what the exact rules were, but we guessed it was to ensure there wouldn't be more men than women in the place. In the end, it didn't work out. We never visited that "museum," and I never had another chance to be so close to going to a swingers' club in my life with a guy that I really liked. Oh well, life goes on.

Last time I heard Mike #1, he texted me after almost a year of no communication and offered to meet at a local cantina in downtown Issaquah, a place I loved to visit on a weekly basis, with a new date every time. He offered to meet in two hours. I agreed and was very excited to see him after such a long time. A lot of things had happened to me since the last time we had met. I was about to move to my new place, a condo in north Seattle. I had finally sold the big house in the middle of the forest and found a beautiful cozy place of my own, and I was very proud of it. I was also still recovering from a lousy health condition that was taking forever to heal, and I was wearing a foot sandal for a few months after an operation on my toes. I wasn't in the best mood, but the anticipation of seeing Mike #1 in a couple of hours made me feel good and happy. I wanted to make sure I looked my best and looked forward to a fun evening with him.

Mike #1 was a delightful person who had diverse experiences in his life. His first child had been born when Mike was eighteen, and he raised his kids from that very young age. He also had different hobbies. He had never travelled out of the United States' borders, but he was very eager to learn and was reading a lot about other places in the world, politically and geographically and sexually. Bringing Mike #1's image to my mind always made me feel ready for sex—immediately. Mike #1 loved to find anecdotes about sexual phenomena around the world. He mentioned the issues of sexual child abuse awareness many times and was very passionate about the subject. It was too much for me, and I had to stop his information eagerness whenever he started talking to me about it. I once asked him if his interest came from a personal place of abuse. Mike #1 never answered this question.

To prepare for our date, I took a scorching steamy shower and made sure I smelled good. I applied Orna 19—my favorite body lotion, which I kept importing from Israel whenever I was visiting there. A small local brand.

I discovered the body lotion when I served in the IDF. It used to be very popular and was sold in the base's cantina. Later on came an international brand name, and its glory days were gone. I stayed loyal. I felt very feminine and sexy when I wore it. Yes, even back then, eighteen years old and dressed up in Israeli's air-force uniform.

Every time I wore the lotion, people complimented me on it. I used it very seldom. As I said, it was only available in Israel. I always noticed how the lucky guy who was with me on a date sniffed it from my neck. Loved this feeling!

It was a nice April evening, so light clothes were more than fine. I hate to dress up in coats and sweaters, something I brought with me after living for eight years in Montreal. Cold weather is not my thing, and two hundred layers always makes me feel fat. For eight winters in Montreal, every time I had to get out of the house/office/store/you name it and face the weather, I felt as if I was not walking, instead, I was rolling. Like a snowball. The weather was a huge part of our relocation to the west coast. Seattle was my Hawaii.

Back to the future hot steamy date!

I needed to choose what to wear, and it had to be the "First impression does count" look. No doubt how I wanted the evening to end.

I chose my winning black shirt, which had a beautiful open shoulder design and a deep cleavage option if I decided to make it that way. I decided to. Buttons stayed open and showed a little of my black lace bra.

I was never heavy on the makeup, so the whole process took me about thirty minutes to get ready, including the shower. I had more than enough time to relax with about an hour before I needed to leave.

I decided to text Tina, just a few words: "Hey, guess who I am meeting in about an hour?" Tina answered me promptly with Mike#1's name. Shoot. She knew me too well. If she will not be my best friend, I'll have to kill her. Tina had met Mike #1 more than once in the past couple of years and had enjoyed long conversations with him about many subjects. She liked him very much and was interested to hear what had happened to him during the time that had passed since our last meeting. I promised to update her after I saw him.

"So," she texted me, "are you planning more than a drink with him?"

"Of course," came my answer.

My last relationship had ended a few weeks earlier, and a date with a kind ex-boyfriend was a great idea. I still carried good memories from our first night together, and from other nights and mornings that we managed to have afterwards. What happened with Mike #1 stayed with Mike #1. And Tina.

When I finally made my way out, it was pouring rain and my travel time just increased by ten minutes. This is Seattle, nothing surprising, and much better than snow. This thought always came to my mind when it rained. This is what eight winters in Montreal had done to me. I hate to be late, so I texted Mike #1 to let him know. His answer was, "Just get there safe." *No hurry*, I thought while I lit a cigarette in my car. He would not go anywhere without me.

Once I parked my car on the other side of the street from the cantina, I had to wait for traffic to quiet before I could run across the street. Jay-walking during a pouring rain is even more dangerous. I know I know, I should not be jay-walking, but I was eager to meet Mike #1. Slipping in the middle of the street was not part of my plan—yes, it had happened before. More than once. I had no coat with me and an umbrella was not something locals carried in Seattle. I do believe what doesn't kill us makes us stronger, and I also believe that we are not made of sugar. Or something else that starts with an S.

When I finally crossed the street, and arrived at the cantina's door, I saw a pudgy man making the same trip as me, and he looked kind of funny. I felt sorry for him getting so wet, so I held the door and waited for him. He got to the door, held it for me now, smiled and said, "Good evening." I answered with a short "good evening," gave him a small smile, and walked inside.

I looked carefully around, trying to find Mike #1. I knew him and knew he would be seated in the bar. I took a good look. About five guys sat there, and some of them smiled at me. I know. I looked hot. Nope, he was not there. But the pudgy guy was still behind me, and I moved out of his way.

"Good evening," I heard him say again, so I was sure I was in his way, and I moved a little more away from the door. I then quickly turned around to see if I was still blocking him. I suddenly felt as if I couldn't breathe. My eyes opened very wide, and a feeling of choking came over me. The man behind me was Mike #1! I saw his face clearly, and the only thought was, "What the hell happened to you?"

I pulled myself together in no time, hoping he hadn't noticed my reaction. Really? I just ignored him for five whole minutes. I hugged him warmly and smiled.

We got a table and faced each other with a small piece of wood between us. I really didn't date Mike #1 outside the bedroom much, so this was only our fourth time that we had sat and talked. Mike #1 ordered a straight tequila—it's a Mexican cantina and a really cool place—and two dishes. I ordered a Sangria. I have visited the place many times, and I know their Sangria is great and generous. I needed some long sips at that moment. My throat was still not back to itself after the surprise I just had. When the drinks and food arrived, things looked better. We exchanged life stories and updated each other on what had happened to us since the last time we met each other a year before.

Mike #1 had gone through a lot, and most of it was not good. He struggled with personal issues, mostly with his older daughter who was nineteen, and it had taken a big toll on his health. He stopped visiting the gym and had been depressed for a long time. I knew how it felt, and my heart went out to him. And then he ordered another dish and told me that he was saving money for another tattoo. He had an amazing one on his chest that had looked great when he was in better shape. I hated the thought of how it might look now.

Mike #1 had moved to a new place and shared an apartment with a good friend of his, so he had someone close to him to make sure he was doing okay. Or at least not doing worse. He asked me if I wanted to see the place, which was a five minutes' drive away. I agreed.

His place was neat, clean, and cozy. It kind of felt like home. His roommate was a bartender, so the place was equipped with the best alcohol you could ask for, and the apartment was empty. Mike #1 knew how to make some good drinks, so we took some time for this before we sat down and continued our discussion.

But things were not the same, and we both knew it. We tried to revive something that was natural and good when it happened, but it was so gone. Although it had been only a year since we had last met, we had traveled completely different journeys and were different people than we were when we first met.

I left his place and drove back home, hoping that I hadn't had too much to drink, and praying not to be stopped by the police. I just wanted to get to my bed and forget this evening. It was a sad one.

He will always be my Mike #1. I met him when I had started my new life. He was the one who showed me what I could expect in my future. This great experience with him brought me to sign onto different online dating sites and made me feel as if I could do whatever made me feel good. The concept for *Around Seattle in 80 Dates* had started from a very good place. I loved how he made me feel and understood that I could choose to feel like this for the rest of my life.

I never heard from him again.

3 - A COUGAR IN GOA

Traveling alone is different when you are a single, mature blonde woman.

For the first time in three decades, I was on a trip as a free woman. I had spent the past thirty-two years of my life with the same guy. I'd just celebrated my forty-seventh birthday, and I felt as if the world was falling apart. My husband and I had recently separated, and I knew that as soon as I returned, we would file for divorce.

I saw Mike #1 the night before I left Seattle for a month. We met for a late drink, and he was very excited for me. Mike #1 had never left the States, and we agreed that when I returned, I would help him find a job that included travelling, which meant we had a plan to meet when I returned. I felt so good about myself. All my concerns and tears seemed so ridiculous suddenly. I had made the decision that when I returned from India, I would join an online dating site. And because I like to do things as soon as possible, I had already created an account on Plenty of Fish, but I hadn't published it yet. I was working on my profile. Yes, I took it very seriously. I also had a lot of free time flying from Seattle to Israel, and a week later, to India. So, I also started answering questions on OKCupid. The more the merrier, right?

I arrived in Goa, India, after spending two weeks locked into crazy business discussions and training for different teams in Pune, India. I'd been a project manager and a business analyst for an international IT company for the past fifteen years, which required traveling all over the United States and internationally.

I was determined to enjoy my trip even though India is not Hawaii. These were the thoughts of a person who had never been to India before. Or to Hawaii.

During the previous two weeks, I had been hosted by local friends and toured various areas in India with new people I had met in both Pune and Mumbai. Some of my hosts were coworkers with whom I had worked for a few years, and some of my hosts were complete strangers who I had met in the hotel where I stayed. The family I made friends with invited me to their home in New Mumbai for a weekend visit, and I was happy to accept their generous offer. I soon discovered that my female host had been one of India's beauty queens, and her husband was one of the most successful pharmaceutical manufacturers in India. The trip to their place was five miles from my hotel in Mumbai, and it took two hours to get to there in a local taxi with lots of cows in the way.

Life in India is nothing like life in the Western world. Life is in the face all the time, and there is no way to hide or ignore it. Imagine the noise of a million cars honking, cows walking free everywhere and looking in the windows, and the strong and sharp smells and vibrant colors. Everybody's clothes were colorful. Black is not a color in India. So different from anything I had ever experienced.

Two weeks into the trip, I finished my work and took a week for myself in a local resort, Goa, known as a party area. This area used to be a wild place, with lots of alcohol, weed, mushrooms, and other goodies. These days the beaches are clean with cameras everywhere and policemen who patrol the area. But parties still take place if you really want to be a part of one. I didn't. I just wanted to relax and think about the future. Traveling as a single woman was a new and fascinating experience, and I found myself enjoying every minute of the independence. I was far away from home, nobody knew me, and I had my life to myself. At least for the next six nights.

I arrived in Goa on a Friday afternoon at four after ten hours of traveling. I used local Indian transportation and had not eaten all day. I was exhausted, but at the same time full of adrenalin, and I anxiously awaited my arrival.

The resort looked very different from what I had booked through Expedia. It was in a rural area, the room/cabins looked as if they might collapse at any time, and the small reception hall held nothing to remind me of the photo on their website.

But who cared?

I threw my small suitcase on the bed, not even taking the time to take things out, except my swimming suit and my weed edibles. I had brought a few marijuana edibles from my hometown in Seattle. I saved it all to get to this point of time in Goa. I had not touched any pot for the past three weeks. This would be, literally, a strong experience.

I chewed two edibles "gummy bears," and changed to my swimming suit. I tied a burgundy dupatta—Indian scarf—over my body and slipped into flip flops to complete my beach attire. I picked up my sunglasses, a towel, sunscreen, and more edibles. I was all ready to welcome the peaceful world awaiting me out there. I even had a book in case I became bored. I hadn't read one page yet so far on this journey. But I knew I would finish the book in Goa, right? I was there to relax, and nothing was going to happen.

I counted sixty-nine steps from my rustic Indian shack, while walking through the hotel's beach restaurant, to the minute I placed my feet in the sand. Sixty-nine steps. I double checked. Twenty more to the ocean. All together less than one hundred steps, and one of my favorite numbers—sixty-nine! (I always run numbers in my mind). I was in heaven and assured myself that nothing could go crazy here.

Five minutes later, I was already lying in the sun on one of the many comfy beach chairs on the sand. I ordered a Kingfisher beer. I had heard it was a good local beer that had received many awards during the years. Heineken Brewery is behind them. The waiter asked if I wanted the big one or the regular bottle. Big always sounds good to me.

"Of course, the Big one," I confirmed. I had no idea what it meant, but I always liked Mr. Big from *Sex and the City*. Well, almost always. Maybe it was an omen to meet Mr. Big in India? I smiled at my own joke. I usually make myself smile, but I try not to share my self-amusement when I'm out in public. I have some really crazy thoughts running in my mind, often dirty. Oh well, this is what happens when you are single again and feel good about yourself. I smiled again.

When the beer arrived, I immediately understood why it was called "Big." Big King Fisher was a double sized bottle—650 ml—and it was all mine, just for me.

I was in Goa relaxing, with the sun, blue sky, calm ocean, and one Big Kingfisher that helped two edibles go down smoothly. I still hadn't eaten anything, and it had been eleven hours since I had eaten. I leaned my head back, as it started to feel too heavy to hold upright.

I glanced to my right. It took one glance, and I woke up right away and straightened my position. I sat up and sucked in my tummy—what's wrong with me? What reflex is that?

On my right side, two seats from me, sat a dark, handsome guy, who looked like a Greek God. Well, like an Indian Greek God. A painting. His hair was a little long, and he wore a small swimming suit, just to cover his privates. Very small cover for privates that looked kind of big. He observed me and smiled. I tried to get a better position. I crossed my legs and tucked my belly in a little more, as quickly as I could. I smiled back. From the quick glance, I surmised he was probably in his very early twenties.

There were two free sun chairs between us, and he turned fully toward my side. I closed my eyes for a second and made sure I looked good when I did so. The beer and the edibles kicked in suddenly, and I felt that my eyes were such heavyweights that I might not be able to open them again. Forever. I decided to get addicted to the sun again. I felt like a lizard and turned my face to make sure the warm sun rays touched every inch. I needed to open my eyes, to put on some sunscreen. I felt the Greek-Indian God's eyes following every move I made. "Graceful" crossed my mind at that moment, but I was not sure how my body would cooperate.

Ehhhh…Fuck the sunscreen and fuck the graceful, and with all due respect, the Greek God next to me as well. I just needed to leave my eyes closed and let my mind fly as high as a kite.

It was a little after five, and the sun was starting to go down. January 4, 2014. The edibles had done a great job with the lovely Big Kingfisher, and I completely forgot about the Greek God lying just two beds away from me.

I suddenly heard a deep sexy voice. I opened my eyes slowly while turning toward the voice. I started to smile, and then I stopped. This was not the guy who set two beds from me. This was an entirely different guy.

This guy was in his thirties, looked like a Bollywood star, and had a fabulous British accent, which I'm completely addicted to since I watched early James

Bond/Roger Moore movies. Ouch. My heart almost missed a beat. But it did not, and I found myself irritated. I felt the moment would never repeat itself, but I have a strong feeling of being unaccompanied and wanting to keep it that way. There were too many things that kept interrupting my mindset and the perfect moment I captured a few seconds ago disappeared.

He introduced himself. His name was Mike, and he asked me for my name.

"Mike," I said, while pulling myself into sitting position and turning to him: "I just landed here an hour ago, after ten hours of traveling from the other side of India. I'm tired, and I really want some time for myself alone. So please tell me what you want."

I know, I'm very straight forward sometimes, and not politically correct, sue me for that, but I didn't have all the time in the world, and every minute reminded me how much I dreamed about this moment, and the journey in life I had gone through to get here. I saw my visit to Goa as one of the most exciting and indulgent trips I had ever made, and I had no patience for small talk and guys hitting on me.

Mike just smiled and introduced himself as the owner of a local jewelry store—so from now will call him Jewelry Mike—located not far away. *Aha, soliciting females/clients on the beach.* But he merely wished me a great vacation. Jewelry Mike said that he was sure we would meet again, and finally he left. Sigh. More sun on my face. I put my head back and relaxed. I closed my eyes while letting out a big exhalation. I had to let the air go out. It felt so much better afterwards.

Two minutes later, I sensed somebody standing next to my head as a shadow passed over me and blocked the warm sun. I opened my very heavy lids and saw a local woman standing over me, making lots of noise, while cutting a fresh pineapple into a small plastic bag. Then she handed it over to me. No, *nahin,* in my poor Hindi, I said and waved my hands. I didn't ask to buy any fruit. But she ignored me and started to peel a papaya into another plastic bag and handed it over to me. She smiled and laughed and pointed toward two sun beds away from me. The young Greek God was still sitting there, and now he was looking straight at me and smiling. He had sent the lady with the fruits. How sweet of him, don't you think?

I couldn't refuse this gesture as it would have been rude and inappropriate. I already felt guilty about my last declaration of independence to Jewelry Mike, five minutes earlier.

I decided to be polite. And he looked like a Greek God.

I slowly brought my chair to a sitting position and smiled softly toward the Greek God's direction. The Greek God quickly rose up, and in no time stood next to me, and asked if he could join me. Well, he made some hand movements—not really sure what he said—but I guessed he wanted to join me. Have you ever had the opportunity to speak to a Greek God? I never had, and I was keen to say yes, *haan.* It is a word I had heard a lot in my local workplace in the past two weeks. One thing I learned for sure and very quickly, Indian people do not like to say no. They instead say yes and do whatever they want later. Who said communication is important?

The Greek God sat on the bed next to me, the same bed that Jewelry Mike just left a few minutes before. We shared the fruit in the plastic bags and started a conversation. His name was Mike, but in my mind, he will always be the Greek/Indian God. The Painting.

Mike's English was excellent, and we had a fluent discussion. I was not surprised anymore by the good English spoken by most of the people I had met. India used to be ruled by the British Empire until 1947, and most people still learn the language as part of their school education and even use it more and more, while replacing Hindi or any other local language that is in use in the area they live. I once tried to ask a few people, how to say, "Good morning" in Hindi (and no, it is not *Namaste*. Indian people laughed at me when I said *Namaste*. They explained that word was a Western yoga thing.) As for "Good morning," their answer was the same, again and again. They use "Good morning." They didn't even understand why I was surprised by their answer whenever I heard it. Only one person, who came from a poor village, told me that in his village they greet each other in the morning by saying, "Did you eat today?" That's a literal translation. If the person answered with "yes," it meant that it was a good morning. Completely made sense to me, the one who came from the wealthy, overweight, USA. Right? I said, "thank you," in my mind, to every bite I had that morning.

The Greek God was nineteen years old and a junior in college. He arrived at the resort with a few friends for a vacation—all of them from the same college. This area is very trendy for guys his age, and they take the time to come every year. I also learned, for the first time, that the resort I chose is tailored toward local Indian people and Russian tourists. I suddenly realized that besides me, there were a few other tourist families on the beach as well. I could hear their Russian in the air all around me. I was so focused and taken by the sun and the blue water that I somehow missed all of it. In another quick glance, I noticed that there were at least ten other blond women on sun chairs like mine. Most of them were in their late twenties with big boobs and wore very minimal swimsuits. They were either accompanied by a girlfriend or with a young family with a kid or two. I looked just like them, I thought, except for two facts: I wore a full swimming suit, and I might be double their age. They all wore a bikini, and some of them were topless, with their chests toward the chair, letting their backs get all the sun they could catch. I saw groups of young Indian guys walking on the beach and looking toward where we sat. They looked very excited to see some skin. It is all about geography and culture.

The Greek God was very impressed when I told him I was originally from Israel. Many Israelis travel to this area of the world when they finish their military service in the IDF. Many of them take a break from life for few months, backpacking, hiking, touring, partying like crazy, and eating lots of mushrooms. I had to defer my break, as I got married immediately after my military service, started to work at three jobs, went to college and had to provide for both my new husband and me. Yep, you can't be a head of a household, go to college, and be stoned in India. Wait—what was I saying? Beside the college part—replace it with two kids—here I was the head of a household and stoned in India. I was still double the age of the girls around me. Nothing is perfect.

The Greek God asked me if I wanted to take a walk on the beach. Well, there went my sunbath and quiet time, but how could I say no to this Painting when he looked straight into my eyes? In the meantime, I finished the Big Kingfisher bottle, and the edibles hit their peak. Everything seemed brighter and bluer than ever. The Painting walked next to me and looked even more attractive than thirty minutes earlier when I first laid my eyes on him.

We started walking. I saw two people playing a racketball game on the beach. I got excited, as this was a popular game on Israel's shores. The rackets they used were very specific to Israel and are called matkot—I had never seen anybody else in the world playing it outside of Israel, my homeland. I was raised in a small town next to the Mediterranean Sea—a ten-minute walk, to be accurate, from the condo my family lived in, to the beach—and I was the Queen of Matkot at the local beach. This meant that all the guys wanted to play with me as I had a very mean "serve" that got my opponents right in the belly button if they weren't careful. Yes, I got some blue marks as well at the time. But that day in Goa, I was very excited and felt like I was back at home, thirty years younger (shit, where did time go?), at the beginning of my life. Adding the sound of the Matkot hitting the ball, it all became real. I was seventeen again with a gorgeous nineteen-year-old Greek God next to me. Wait, stop. No, thank you. Love being forty-seven, worked hard for it.

The Painting asked me what I was doing in Goa.

"I'm writing a book," I told him.

"What kind of a book?" the Painting kept asking, while looking at me very seriously now, and I could not hold myself back.

"The sexiest book in the world," I told him. "You think you will want to read it?" I have no idea why I said it. At that point in life, I was not even thinking of writing a book, and the idea for this book came a few months later. But the words just came out of my mouth, and there was no way I could take them back.

The Painting froze for a whole minute. His eyes suddenly became huge, while staring at me. "Yes," he finally said with a loud voice, "of course, I want to read it."

I laughed very hard. "Of course, you do, you and ninety-nine percent of the women and men in the world."

We kept walking, and no words were said. I just kept absorbing all the air I could get, as I felt that my head was getting heavier every second, and I could barely walk. I was very thirsty, tired, and the only thing I wanted to do at that moment was to drop myself on the sand and fall asleep. At that point, it had been twelve hours without any food, except for two edibles and one Big Kingfisher. Oh, and a slice of a pineapple, but I was not sure how clean it had been. I felt something moving in my stomach. I hoped I hadn't swallowed a bug.

Suddenly, the Painting turned around to me, grabbed my hand and said, "Take me to your room."

"What?" I asked amazed. My head started to spin like crazy, and my throat cried for some fluid.

"Take me to your room. I will do anything you tell me to do. I'm a virgin."

Well, I did not expect that for sure, so I told the Painting that I needed to think about it for few minutes, and I walked away from him a little, to be with myself and try to get some order into my thoughts. I knew I wasn't thinking straight, and I needed to review my options.

What the hell. I'm alone, I'm single, high like a kite, which means I'm also horny like crazy, and this Indian/Painting/Greek God next to me has just offered to be my love slave. Hmm... sounds like a yummy idea. I decided to go for it. What happens in Goa, stays in Goa, right?

I walked back to my Indian/Greek God and felt like every step was getting heavier and heavier as if I was sinking in the sand.

"Okay," I said to the Painting while walking toward him, "I agree. Let's go to my room."

The Painting smiled broadly and suddenly was walking very close to me, brushing against my arm gently. His skin was warm and firm and felt good.

While we got closer to the resort, I felt very weird. Everything around me moved too fast. My head was spinning. I needed to sit down, and it needed to happen ASAP. I need to eat and drink something, I thought.

I told the Painting that we were going to stop in the restaurant in front of the hotel, as I wanted to grab some food, and he agreed with a big smile.

We sat down, and the waiter brought the menu. I felt a tremendous need for a bottle of water. The first rule to follow in India religiously is always drink from a NEW and NOT an opened bottle. I asked the waiter to hurry up with the water first, and the server literally ran to bring the water from the kitchen. I forgot how customer oriented the Indian people are. If one asks for something, they will physically run to the market to bring it, as it is not acceptable to say, "Sorry, we ran out of it." I should be careful, I reminded myself, to be gentler, maybe?

Meanwhile, after reading the menu and a short consultation with me, the Painting decided to order the same dish as I had decided to order. Really? I thought, *you could not do better, but order the same thing that I just did?* I hate to share a meal when my partner has the same dish as me. This is an annoying and a boring sign.

When the waiter came back with the water (I learned later, that only men work in the food industry in Goa), I gave him my order. When the Painting started to give his order, I stopped him and asked the waiter to write down my order only and directed him to bring me another bottle of water. I had already finished the first one that he had rushed to bring to me. I thanked the waiter in Hindi (*Dhanyavaad*), and without thinking, asked him to hurry up with the water once again. The waiter ran from the table the minute he finished writing down the order. Whoops, I had done it again.

The server did not give the Painting any sign of recognition and ignored him completely.

The Painting was confused and tried to ask me what is going on. So was I—confused. What the heck was I doing there sitting with a nineteen-year-old kid, about to take him to my room, and he was a virgin!!! Really? Was I an Indian Cougar now? The idea made me smile. Not good—my head spun even more. *No sudden movement*, I thought, *stay calm and don't move anything*.

I turned very slowly toward the Painting and said, "Dear Mike, I'm sorry. I'm very sorry, but you are really young, and I'm not interested in being anybody's teacher. I have a daughter your age. I can't do it, it is not me."

"But why?" the Painting asked. "Don't you like me? Don't you think I'm attractive?"

Boy... attractive is not a word you use for a painting who is also 6' 5" tall and nineteen years old, with an incredible tanned skin and abs. Not to mention the small cover on his private parts that didn't look so small. Did I mention all of this already?

"I just can't," I told him. "Please, just leave. I appreciate you being so nice, and I'm sure you are going to do amazing in school and life. You have the right attitude to succeed."

Why did I give him a motivation speech? Why was I saying all of that? I believe that the motherhood part took over at that point, combined with my Jewish/Polish heritage. Weird, but it is what it is. "Please, just leave, I need to be alone."

Mike left, and I saw him sitting in the far corner of the restaurant watching me. I moved to a different chair, so he was forced to look at my back. I got the second bottle of water, which I drank slowly, and I finished it all. My head was still spinning, and I felt like I couldn't move from the comfy and filthy chair under me. So, I decided to close my eyes. Just for a minute. Until the food arrived. Until the sun moved and stopped gently touching my face between the leafy roof cracks, until my head and my heart stopped pumping so hard, I would just close my eyes for a minute, and then everything would be okay.

I woke up an hour later, still sitting next to the table, and I felt entirely reenergized.

The Painting was still seated on the other side of the restaurant, but he had moved to a different table and was looking straight at me.

I had fallen asleep, in the middle of a restaurant on the beach, and they just let me sleep there.

I hope I hadn't snored. Oh well, can't take first impressions back.

The food was on the table in front of me, and it was cold. I could not ask to warm it, as there were no microwaves, only open-flame ovens. It did not matter, I felt like I could eat a horse, and I just finished it all. The food was fantastic and tasty even though it was cold and mushy. My stomach was now shouting THANK YOU for every bite I put in my mouth. My head had stopped spinning, and I could sit straight and look around me.

It was almost eight o'clock. It had been four hours since I had first set my foot on the beach, my first day in Goa. My first four hours in Goa and so many things already had happened. I reminded myself that I came to relax, absorb as much sun, seafood, and beer as possible while doing nothing while all ALONE. I swear, I smiled and nodded my head to myself. I was far away from Seattle, I didn't need to think about the divorce that waited for me at home, and the Wi-Fi wasn't working on the beach, so I couldn't look at any online dating sites.

Tomorrow was a new day. Jewelry Mike with his British accent might stop by. What happened in Goa would stay in Goa.

4 - ONCE I TRIED GOING BLACK

I have to admit, one of the things on my online dating wish list—it was always on my mind and didn't leave me—was the desire of dating black men.

I was raised in an area of the world, Israel, where the only black men I saw were on TV, usually on *NYPD Blue*, peeking from behind bars.

But I also heard a lot of stories, and I always thought that black men were the best dancers, and this attribute was good enough evidence that they were also great in bed, right?

When I became single, I also heard the phrase, "Once you go black, you never go back." So, I added it to my "to do" list, and I decided I would make sure it was marked as "done." There was a whole new world out there, and I just needed to reach and touch. This was exactly my intention—reach and touch. I wasn't shy, but, of course, it had to be done according to my conditions, which meant that we were having a good time, and I wanted it to happen. By "it," I meant going to bed with a black guy.

The first black man who I dated was shortly after I started online dating. He was from Texas and had just relocated to Seattle for a UPS job. He sounded very nice on the phone, and his texts were polite and flattering. His first question was, "Have you ever dated a black man before?" No, was my answer, and I felt that Mike #9 was very happy with that response. Mike #9 was a great dancer, according to his words on the phone—you see, all black men are great dancers, I told you—and he wanted to take me out dancing. I was happy to join him for that activity but asked for a meet and greet a few days before for dinner, to make sure we really wanted to go dancing together. His birthday was coming, and he was very excited about going out with me.

As he wasn't familiar with my area on the eastside, outside of the city proper, I was in charge of finding a place, and offered an Italian restaurant not far away from me, which I had never visited before. This was my first mistake. Mike #9 agreed, and we scheduled to meet in two days.

At the right time and day, I parked my car next to the restaurant, when Mike #9 called my cell. He was stuck in traffic and would be fifteen minutes late. I assured him not to worry and asked him to drive safely. The Italian restaurant was nested in a cute little street mall, and the shops were all local boutiques. I took my time to wander around the area.

Mike #9 arrived at the restaurant thirty minutes later— after five more phone calls. He sounded very upset and nervous with the traffic and the unfamiliar route. In his last call, he made me stay with him on the line, reading every road sign he saw on his way, making sure he was headed in the right direction, and yelling when he thought he was lost. Not very attractive, I have to admit. Oh well, he finally arrived, and I was ready to start this date.

We walked into the place and found ourselves in a cozy little Italian restaurant, very romantic and very quiet. No, we didn't have reservations—it was a Wednesday night, for Christ sake, in Issaquah—and we were seated at a nice table for two, with people sitting at every table around us. The place was small, and we could hear part of discussions from the tables next to us.

We got the menus and started our search. When the waiter came back with the water and some fresh rolls and butter, Mike #9 had already read the menu, and asked me, very loudly, what kind of a place was it, that charged eighteen dollars for meat balls and tomato sauce? I choked a little, and suggested he choose a different dish, maybe? Mike #9 declared that he was not eating all the other things, and meat balls looked like the best and only choice for him. But eighteen dollars? Boy, from where he came this was an eight-dollar dish. *Nice going*, I thought, *this is going to be an interesting evening.*

I ordered a glass of the house red, a Cabernet Sauvignon, and made a note to myself that I would pay for my own dinner. Mike #9's drink was a rum and coke. He was okay with the drink he got, although the price at twelve dollars seemed very high to him.

Our discussion went into relocation between places, getting used to roads, and adjusting to prices of different services. Mike #9 had just been promoted in his job with UPS, and in order to take over the new position, he was asked to relocate to Seattle. He had arrived four months earlier and lived in SeaTac, our local airport city, and he informed me he was really interested in having a lady friend who he could take care of. The definition of "taking care of" was very broad and included a lot of "honey" and "sweetheart" phrases. Mike #9 also knew how to sing, and at one point he started singing to me, while we waited for our food to arrive. He was really a good singer, and the people from the other tables clapped their hands when he was done. He sang, "Good girl – I Know You Want It," by Robin Thicke. I smiled, blushed a little, and enjoyed my time. So, this was what it meant to date a black guy. This was fun. We finished our dinner. I paid half of the bill, and Mike #9 looked very happy. We decided to continue to a wine bar that I frequented, less than a mile drive away. I knew there was a ladies' meetup taking place there that night, along with a music performance, blues style. Mike #9 loved the idea.

We arrived while the band played their last notes. My meetup girlfriends all cheered and clapped their hands when we walked in the door. This was a hell of a white drunk group of crazy women, the audience was all white, the band was all black, and so was my date. There were no other black people in the bar. Mike #9 approached the band when they were done, and they "hi-fived" some kind of a hand shake, which until then,

I had seen only in the movies. Another cool thing, I marked on my list of dating a black guy, adding another plus.

My lady friends were very happy to see us and insisted we sit with them at their table. The investigation started. The first question: How long have you known each other? The answer: two hours. They were very amused to hear that. He knew how to flatter and gave attention to each one of them, with his deep manly voice and his "honey" words. They were all falling in love with him. A few of them took me aside to tell me how handsome he was and that I should go for it. I completely agreed and promised them I would follow their advice.

Mike #9 and I went out for a smoke. Smokers have a lot of alone moments. While we were out, Mike #9 sang again the song about the good girls, and how he knew I wanted it. I was completely on the same page with him, and I even let him kiss me at one point before we said goodbye. He was a great kisser.

The next couple of days passed with a lot of funny text messages and compliments about my looks and conversation. Mike #9 looked forward to our Saturday night date, which was a very special evening for him—his fifty-third birthday. Mike #9 insisted on picking me up from my hometown, although his place was closer to the dancing club, and he would have to travel an extra hour. What a gentleman, I thought, and agreed to meet him in the same parking lot where we met the first time—next to the eighteen-dollar meatballs Italian restaurant—

this was how we referred to the place since our dinner there. It was our joke, and we laughed about it together.

All I knew about the club, was that it is in Hilton SeaTac, on the fourteenth floor, and it played R&B music. Cool, sounded different from the gay clubs I'd been visiting lately and the awful music they had. House techno. All the songs had the same beat—everything sounded the same—boring. But the crowd was always interesting.

The big day arrived. Saturday night. Mike #9 picked me, this time right on time. He looked very sharp, wearing a neat suit and smelling amazing. He was smooth and full of compliments, while trying to hold me next to him, despite the fact he was driving on a highway at night. I let him hold my hand, just to stop the battle on the road, and he kept kissing and fondling it. It was somehow embarrassing and uncomfortable. He kept talking about his birthday, and how happy he was to be with me. He said I was the woman of his dreams, and maybe I would give him his best birthday present ever.

I chose to ignore this sentence.

We entered the elevator for the club on the fourteenth floor, and with us entered a gang of people, all black and all are dressed sharp from head to toe. If somebody would have asked me, how does a pimp dress, I would definitely point at half of them. There is a men's clothing store on Pike Street downtown Seattle, that sold these kinds of clothes. Shoes as well. The ties were amazing with strong pink, purple and yellow colors. The suits were colorful, and they came in crazy colors, but purple was always my favorite. I thought every time I passed the store, *who wears a yellow suit?* and was drawn to look at the store's window with a yellow suit always on display. I never saw the place open during all the times I passed it—usually lunch time. I always wondered who the clientele was. Now I knew. I smiled. They were all standing in the elevator with us.

Mike #9 saw me smiling and decided that he had to hug me even harder and pulled me closer to his body. All the guys in the elevator looked at him with a big smile of appreciation. *Wow, I feel like a piece of jewelry.* The way that women looked at each other's jewelry and commented, this is how those men were looking at me and smiling at Mike #9. Well, I'm forty-seven, and this was not bad timing to boost my confidence. "Never say never," ran through my mind at that point.

The club was packed, and we had a table reserved next to a huge window that showed the whole city and some of the airport. People were dressed up—all of them. There were no jeans. "Dress to Impress" was the theme. I knew I looked good, and I was also one of the few white blonde women around. Natural blonde, it is. Okay, let's stay with the white. I was one of the few white women in the club, most of them were much older than me and not natural blondes. Looking closely, they were all dressed up in small tight black dresses and could hardly move on their high heels. They were drinking constantly, and it looked like they knew everybody in the club.

I was wearing a mini black skirt and a sleeveless shirt with a small cleavage. I love to dance and get hot and sweaty very quickly. Besides a thin elegant coat, I had nothing else to wear. I also don't wear high heels, as my toe had gone through a few surgeries lately, and it ended my high heels career forever. I know, life sucks.

Mike #9 and I sat down, captured the surroundings, and got hooked to the beat of the music. He still held my hand, very tightly. He was looking around and made eye contact with different guys sitting near us. I noticed the head nods, the smiles, and the thumb-up sign, from some guys. Yup, I was checked out, by multiple men at the same time, while the guy next to me was taking ownership of me. It made me smile. I had never been in a situation like this, where so much testosterone was around and being *shpritzed*—Yiddish for squirt— everywhere. Ouch, I got some in my eye.

After another quick look around the room and using my analytic mind, I calculated percentages, something I always did. It looked like ninety-nine percent of the men in the room were black, and I could say, almost the same about the women's proportion. The odds in the room were 3:1. Three men for every woman. This meant that I was very special, a rare commodity.

I understood why Mike #9 was eager to hold my hand and why he took ownership of me in a very strong and "show off" way.

Ten minutes later, we were still sitting next to the window and holding hands. Well, Mike #9, held my hand, while I tried to take my hand away. I suggested we have a drink. As no waiter was around, I got up and started walking to the bar. My hand was now finally free.

My date followed very close behind me with his hand over my waist. Touching, but very softly. I had no complaints; his touch was soft and firm. I felt like I was being walked by him, a little pushed. Again, a new feeling for me, and I liked it.

We arrived at the bar, and I offered to buy Mike #9 a drink, as this was his birthday. He happily agreed. Very happily. I paid for our drinks, a local beer for me. Mike #9 had a very interesting combination of the best rum in the house and some whipped cream and coconut. A fourteen-dollar drink. I hoped it was as good as it cost. I wished Mike #9 the best luck in the coming year, while toasting with our drinks. When we got back to our table, the dance floor was already full. I loved it! So many people danced with lots of guys by themselves—until they found women to hit on—and big cool black mamas. Next to them, I felt like a petite skinny woman—again, a new feeling for me. This was the first time in my life that I didn't have the biggest boobs in the room. I know, crazy, right? And they were all real and came with a large big black figure, accompanied by a really big sticking-out butt, all wrapped in very tight outfits. Some of the ladies were dancing so slow, while their bodies floated around the floor. Beautiful sights to capture. I noticed the stories starting to take place on the dance floor—who was approaching who, who was saying no, who touched where. I loved people watching. Mike #9 was now again holding my hand when I forgot to hold the beer bottle for a second.

"Let's dance," Mike #9 said, and I took off my jacket in a second. I was ready. I wore a short black mini skirt, with lace stockings. My blouse was half see-through, and my very small heels were not much of a help now with all the tall people around us. But I loved to dance, the music was R&B, and it's crazy, but I suddenly felt right at home.

Mike #9 was a good dancer, and also—as I knew already—a good singer. He sang in my ears while we danced. We really did a good job on the dance floor, and people gave us room, and clapped their hands as they surrounded us.

The DJ suddenly announced Mike #9's birthday and greeted him, while the crowd burst with applause. *Didn't he just move here?* I thought. It was either a very friendly crowd, or something was going on. We got back to our table, finished our drinks, and I suggested that we go and get another drink. The ceremony repeated itself with Mike #9 behind me, touching my waist, kind of pushing/protecting me from the crowd. When we got to the bar, he stood behind me. Now I get it. He was expecting me to buy him drinks all night. Oh well, this was going to be a short night then.

We danced a little more, and then we went out for a smoke, which meant back with our jackets and coats— it's February and I don't have a coat—a quick sip from our drinks and back to the elevator. From floor fourteen down to ground. We had to look for a place to smoke. It's funny how people who smoke have this special bonding between them; it's like starting from a common ground.

Stinky, but something that you enjoy, and now most of the world does not. Now we have "Smokers" against the rest of a world that doesn't smoke. Bonding time for us.

I dropped myself gently into Mike #9's lap, trying not to put all my weight on him. I was freezing, and I found it hard to resist his hug. We kissed a little, and I congratulated him with a "Mazal Tov," to which he paid me back with a strange look, as if I just said a bad word. I had to explain to him what the term meant, and he relaxed and kissed my hand. He was trying to make out with me a little further and deeper, but I noticed cameras above us, and I asked him to stop before we became an item with the security guys at the hotel. I'm sure these guys saw a lot of couples, who never noticed the cameras, making out on this bench. Mike #9 didn't care. Of course, he didn't. He would be proud if our session went viral. I didn't share this feeling, so I stood up and walked back to the elevator, not looking behind.

When the elevator's door opened, it was filled to its max with guests coming down! All of the people inside the elevator were black people, dressed up amazingly, and drunk. They were all very happy, and the ladies were the first to get out from the elevator because the men were well-mannered. The women were all jerking on their very high heels, and were very tipsy, with loud talking and lots of laughing. When the men got out of the elevator, they looked very happy as well, and each one of them took the time to have a "high-five," or other handshake with Mike #9, who stood next to me. He hugged me and attached me to his body very closely and hard. His smile was something else. I never ever saw a man smiling like that. Oh well, happy birthday, I thought. It's going to end soon, so enjoy it while you can.

We got back to the club, and I bought us the third round. It looked like there was no chance Mike #9 would take his wallet out. Might be a cultural thing that I'm not aware of? I knew that my girlfriends would cover everything on my birthday, so I guessed that this was what was happening here. Oh well. It was his birthday, and I didn't want to spoil the moment, but I wasn't feeling comfortable with me buying all the drinks. I had brought some cash, and after the third round, I was out of money. I hadn't brought any plastic cards with me, so if something went wrong, I was stuck. I wasn't happy with these thoughts.

Two hours later, we both were tipsy when we got to Mike #9's car. It was almost one o'clock, and we had about a forty-minute drive. I had another twenty-minute drive after Mike #9 dropped me. I couldn't wait to get to my car and get home. I was tired and thirsty for water. I danced the whole night, and I could feel my toe crying for help.

I let Mike #9 put his hand on my leg while he drove and talked nonstop. He told me how he was going to take care of me, how he was going to be my man and protect me, and how he could move to my place, and how he didn't mind leaving his place behind. Mike #9 also calculated how much I made as a project manager in an IT company and said that we would have enough money to take short trips to Vegas and cruises—I hate Vegas, and I have never been on a cruise. Mike #9 assured me he had everything under control, and he promised to take over my life like a real man. I sat there and listened to his amazing deep voice and felt as if I was in the middle of an episode from a movie that would soon be over. I was taking Improv classes at that time, and every situation in life suddenly became an Improv moment.

I loved Improv because I was served with a suggestion/offer where the other person would say/do something, and I was allowed/expected to take it anywhere I wanted. It required listening closely to get the suggestion/offer and embrace it. It was up to me how and what was going to happen. There were no rules.

I turned to Mike #9 and removed his hand from my leg. I held it with both my hands and said, in a very gentle voice, "Oh, Mike #9, no guy has ever said anything like that to me. It was always my dream to hear those words from the man who will be my husband."

Mike #9 loved it. He gave me a big smile and continued talking about our mutual future, where we would live together, where he would take care of me, and where he would be my man—a man of only one woman. He made me promise to him that I was a one man's woman. I agreed and promised him that I was a one man's woman, have always been. He loved it and continued talking about our future. And Vegas.

Mike #9 gave me a long hot kiss before I left the car. He didn't get out to escort me to mine. Mike #9 drove away before I reached my car. He did text me fifteen minutes later to tell me he was on the highway, and there were police cars everywhere. He hoped he wouldn't be pulled over, as we drank too much, because I kept buying him drinks. "Good night, Mike," I texted him back, "safe drive."

I got home, took a quick shower and went to bed. I was tired from dancing and was amused from what had just happened in the car. Was this how black man behaved when they met a woman they liked? This "I am your man" thing? I fell asleep hearing Mike #9's voice in my head, singing "I know you want it."

When I woke up the next morning, I immediately remembered everything that had happened the night before and felt weird. I felt as if I was in a game, and somebody was trying to play me, while I was not playing back. I never liked these kinds of behaviors—taking over me—and texted Tina to tell her what had happened.

In the meantime, I got three text messages from Mike #9. He wished me a good morning, and said he was very busy that day. Then he asked what I was doing and when could he see me again. Overwhelming was an understatement to how I felt. I added this information to Tina, so she could get the whole picture. TMI is not the case here. We were analyzing a situation, and she needed all the details. A war room was just created.

Tina texted me right away and ordered me to tell the poor guy that this was not going to work, and that I was sorry if I was misunderstood. She called him "a good guy," "a man who is looking for a woman." She told me I was a bad person for playing with people's feelings. She advised me to say it in a phone call and not on a text message.

Okay, okay. I agreed with her. I promised to call him and say I was sorry and goodbye. I texted Mike #9—it was Sunday morning—and asked him if he was free for few minutes to speak on the phone. He called me right away. Did I mention already he had an amazing deep voice? Just the way he said "sweetie" made me smile. I let him finish his good morning greetings and told him that I needed to say something very important and needed his full attention as he was falling around and about to start to sing a song. I told Mike #9 that I had had a really nice time at the club the night before, and I was very thankful that he introduced me to this place. I knew I was going back there for sure! But I did wonder who I would be taking with me? A new plan had just started in my mind. But now I need to deal with Mike #9.

I asked him if he had had a good time, too, and he said he had. Then I complimented him on his dancing moves and voice.

And then I said, "Mike, you are an amazing man, but I just separated from my husband, and I am not looking for a relationship right now. I'm sure you understand. I will be happy to go dancing as friends, sometime, if you feel like it."

It took Mike #9 a few seconds to answer me. He said that of course he understood, that I needed to have my time, and he wished me all the best. Wow, it went very well. He was a real *mensch*—Yiddish for a person with integrity, honorable, and he had taken it very gracefully.

He was really one of the good guys.

I texted Tina, assuring her that all had gone fine. Tina texted me back and said she was happy I was honest and finished it quickly.

And then hell broke loose, and shit hit the fan.

The first message came thirty minutes after we finished our call from the site where we met—a Facebook "Singles in Seattle" page. The message, "You are fake boobs." I read it on my phone, so it was small, and I couldn't really see much. I laughed. How does he know I have fake boobs? One of the things that I'm really proud of is that everything in my body is naturally mine. My boobs are one of my—literally—biggest physical assets. How did he dare say something like that about me? I almost cried I was laughing so hard. And then I opened my laptop and saw his message again: "You are a fake babe." Oh, this made so much more sense. I loved it when he used the babe word. Made me feel like a child for a second.

The next message from Mike #9, ten minutes later, was a text message, as he had my phone number, right? I dated him twice already, and we were texting for few days before we met. In his text messages, he said that he was going to say the same, that it was not going to work between us and that he wished me all the best. Okay, I thought, he was angry and now he was back to himself, or something like that. We were good and done.

Fifteen minutes later, I got another text message, and this time it included an attachment—a picture of him, standing next to a beautiful Caucasian petite woman.

They were hugging and posing for a photo. He said that this was his wife, and when he got back home yesterday, a message waited for him from her. She wanted to try again. He said they had two kids, and they owed it to them. They talked on the phone until four in the morning, and he was about to tell me all about it, just before I asked to speak to him. He was not divorced, as he first presented himself, he was only separated.

I texted him back, saying that I completely understood and told him how lucky he was, and wished him all the best in the world. He texted back in response that I was a selfish bitch, and I would always be alone. At this point, I blocked him.

I told my friend, Maxine, about this experience. She is happily married to a very cool black man. She has been married three times, all of them to black guys. She is 6' 2" tall, white, classy, and dresses up all the time like she is about to go out to the most elegant place in the world. Always perfect makeup and high heels.

I saw Maxine as my authority for black men. Maxine told me that many black guys go out to the "market" as divorced, while they have a wife and kids waiting for them at home. "It can't be," I told her. "He took me to a public place, and everybody saw us together." Maxine laughed hard.

"Sweetie," she said, "these guys don't tell about each other. They are all in it together."

Then she added, "Don't buy a drink or spend money on a black guy. They are not used to it from black women. When a white woman offers to pay, and they agree, it is a sign for them that you have money, and they need to help you to spend it."

That was a harsh thing to hear, so I thanked Maxine and thought that she was indeed going too far with her views. Oh well, it was only the first black guy I had dated, so I wasn't going to generalize now about all the black guys, and I did want to date a black guy and enjoy his company, and some other benefits that I heard black guys have. I decided that I needed to continue my quest.

A couple of months later, I was approached by a few black men, but there was no chemistry in the text messages or discussions on the phone. They were very aggressive from the first text or call and called me "baby" from the first sentence. One of them had a beautiful picture wearing dark glasses on the online Plenty of Fish site. We got into a discussion on the web, until he asked me for my phone number. I gave my phone number to the new Mike Sunglasses.

A couple of hours later, I received a text message from Mike Sunglasses. He was distraught with me and had a damn good reason. I had given him, by mistake I swear, my ex-husband's phone number—in my defense, we have one-digit difference between us, so fat fingers are bound to happen. He CALLED the number, and my ex-husband answered and gave him my correct phone number right away, with no questions.

I apologized like crazy. I went back to my original message and saw my mistake. This was sooooo embarrassing. I promised Mike Sunglasses that it was a fat fingers mistake, and in no way, was it intended—my subconscious must have been involved, so sue me! Mike Sunglasses accepted my apology and gave me a long lecture. The lecture was about how he understood from this incident that we were a close family with a one-digit difference, and that my ex-husband was not cautious about my personal information or very smart, and just gave my phone number away to a stranger. I couldn't dispute the intelligent comment. Mike Sunglasses had a soft, calm voice, and many times during the call, he asked me to hold on to listen to him and hear his thoughts. He had a lot of opinions and conclusions about who I was and how I managed my life. He thought that I was under stress—Oh God, I only typed one wrong digit—and that I might still be thinking about my ex-husband.

I was more than a little turned off by his analysis and conclusions that went too far, but I still felt guilty about giving the wrong phone number and played along. He "smelled" my guilt and continued with the discussion— and he wasn't even Jewish! I just listened. At the end of his lecture, he said that he needed to go to work, even though it was four p.m., but he said he would call me later in the day, and maybe I would like to have a late drink with him. We agreed to touch base around 8:30. I told him that the thought of a late drink was very welcome in my eyes. His last question, "Have you ever dated a black guy before?" I admitted I hadn't.

Mike Sunglasses called at 9:30—and yes, I was waiting and hadn't planned anything else. I stayed home for him. He didn't apologize for the lateness and just said that he was stuck at work because the guy who was supposed to replace him called in sick. I understood entirely. I've been in situations like this more than once and promised him that it was okay. Mike Sunglasses couldn't talk much and didn't answer my question about where he worked so late.

The next day, Mike Sunglasses texted to tell me he would text me the next day around five p.m., and maybe I would like to go out for dinner later. He did call, at 6:30 p.m., didn't mention a word that he had asked me out for dinner, and told me that he had to go to work and would call me when he was done. Mike Sunglasses asked me to take a picture of myself and send it to him. Just a photograph of how I looked at that moment. I had guys asking this before—a picture from right then. I think it is a way for them to be reassured the images they saw online were for real. I had no issue cooperating and was happy to text him a picture and asked him to do the same. It was 6:30 at night in April and dark. He texted me a picture of him with dark sunglasses, face only. He had a nice profile and really elegant sunglasses. What was he hiding there? Was he cross-eyed? I didn't say a word. He told me that he worked two jobs. I've always had a weakness for guys who work hard. I appreciated, in general, people who work hard. I still didn't know what the two jobs were. But at least he worked hard, right? I, again, wished him a good "day" at work, as he said he would be finishing at three a.m. But the next night he was free, and he really wanted to see me. I promised him that I would be happy to devote the next evening to him.

Mike Sunglasses called three days later, and I didn't answer. He left a message and asked me to call back. Did I mention already that he had an incredibly deep sexy voice? Well, he did, but at that point, I had lost my interest and my guilt toward him about the wrong number. Playing games was never part of my strategy. I decided not to return his call.

I got another text message from him a few hours after his last text message. Mike Sunglasses didn't understand what was going on and wanted to know why I was playing hard to get. He said he had cleared his evening to take me out. I didn't answer.

Two days afterwards, I got another text message from Mike Sunglasses, asking if we could start all over again, and that he really wanted to see me. I answered him back with one word: "Why?" "Why what," he replied. "WHY do you want to see me?" I asked him.

I never heard from Mike Sunglasses again.

Well, there were different men out there, so there went another episode, I thought, and I still wanted to date a cool black man! No prejudice from my side and no generalizing.

When Mike Limo reached out to me, on OKCupid, I saw a *very* handsome black man, with great pictures and some interests that we shared. No sunglasses. I was more than happy to schedule a date with him. Mike Limo was very intrigued by the fact that I was a storyteller and a standup comedian. He told me he had never been to a storytelling event. I suggested I get us tickets to a storytelling show in downtown Seattle at a very cool

He said he never had experienced this before and that black women never made a gesture like that. I assured him that it was more than okay, and I was very happy to do this for him. In the back of my mind, Maxine's words popped up. She had a point, and I now got it. Then Mike Limo asked me if I had ever dated a black guy before. No, I confessed again, besides going out dancing once with a black guy, I had never dated a black guy. This was the third time he had asked me the same question, and it sounded like he wanted to reassurance about my answer and choose his move accordingly.

A glance at the check showed a total bill of eighteen dollars. Mike left a two-dollar tip. Oh well, I had lived in Canada, and bad tipping was part of my legacy, so I didn't say a word, just left another two dollars when he walked away and waited for me at the front door.

We walked into the theater, and it suddenly hit me. Mike Limo was the only black guy there. Perhaps I should say the only black person. I suddenly noticed the way he looked around him, and even the way he walked. It all changed. It seemed as if he was under some stress. I gave him his space.

I met a few people who I knew from other storytelling events, introduced Mike Limo as a friend, and had some small talk while waiting for the show.

Off Jackson Theater has a very fun décor. The seats are a combination of all kinds of sofas and chairs, not very traditional or formal. You can choose to sit on a couch and have your partner next to you in a very cozy homey way. You can choose to sit next to a table, with few chairs around it, as if you were sitting in a backyard at a friend's house. The stage stands very close to the audience, and the whole room is small and intimate. The bar is basic and holds some hard alcohol and beers. Nothing fancy. The prices are very reasonable. Six dollars for hard liquor and four dollars for a local beer. The selection included cheap and basic items that everybody knew. Mike Limo was so happy with the prices. We stood together in line, and he paid for his drink and waited for me to pick my drink and pay for it. Whoops, this was not a good sign. Maxine and her talk, again, popped into my mind.

We sat down on a comfy old couch, and the show started. The stories were diverse with different themes and people, but none of them were black-oriented. I felt Mike Limo looking around the whole evening. What was he looking for? It seemed he did not feel comfortable in the setting. Well, too late, we were there, and the show goes on.

At the end of the show, Mike Limo walked me to my car. He was without a car that day and had to take a bus back home, which took him almost two hours.

I thanked him for coming and for dinner and drove away. Not for me, I remembered thinking. Four roommates, no car, and he didn't offer to buy a six-dollar drink for his date. This was not my dream.

Mike Limo texted the next day, thanked me for the show, and asked if I would be free in the coming days. I apologized and said I already had plans, including the weekend, and would not be available to see him. Maybe the next week. Mike Limo got the hint very fast. His next text message was, "You have my number, and if you are looking for a good time, give me a call." I never talked to him again.

I still wanted to date a black guy. Okay, I have to confess. I wanted to go to bed with a handsome black man and see if all the stories I had heard had a case.

So, I continued my search.

Mike Jr.—he had three names and reading them sounded like he was from an English royal family. He was a PR professional, and according to his words, "He is the only black person in the Seattle who owns a PR firm." He had a good strong picture with sunglasses. Again, I thought, what's with those dark sunglasses? What was HE hiding behind? His other pictures showed him at official events, wearing a suit and a tie and wearing sunglasses. I love a man in an elegant suit. It does it to me, I admit. We chatted for few days on the web, until we decided to meet for a cup of coffee in Renton. Top Pot Donuts was the destination. I hated donuts, but Mike Jr. did not ask me and just told me. I said yes, as I knew that at least it meant that I wasn't going to eat anything—these dates made me gain weight. Wine and food every day is nice, but also dangerous for your diet. Here I said it—I was worried about my weight. I hated to complain about my diet when I had so much fun.

The area that Mike Jr. chose was a new area in Renton, where massive building efforts were taking place. The city was changing, and I found myself in the middle of a huge street mall with an open shopping area and tons of shops and restaurants. I was not a big fan of places like that because they all looked the same to me with no character or charm. Oh well, America. The same shit different states. Oh, Canada. I had the same views there.

This place could as well have been in the middle of Monroe, Louisiana. It looked and felt identical, with different people who looked the same, only the accent and slang was different.

Top Pot is one of the places that always made me smile. Where did they come with a name like that? Later on, I learned that it was originally supposed to be named Top Spot. Two brothers started the business from Capitol Hill in Seattle. The brothers bought a vintage neon sign that belonged to a Chinese restaurant called TopsPot. While traveling with their new neon sign, the "S" fell off. So now, they had a Top Pot sign.

When I looked at this, I imagined Pot. You know, like weed, marijuana, you name it. The first time I saw the sign, a few months ago, I just started laughing and took a picture. I thought it was a joke. Thank you, Wikipedia, for clarifying this.

It was a Friday early in the evening, and the area was packed with families shopping, and people enjoying their time. The dining selection was large and interesting. Moreover, between all these diverse food and drink places, my future date chose the Top Pot. Oh well, plans can always change. I decided not to go into Top Pot—I hate the smell of dounts—and waited outside to see who was the guy that I was about to have a date with. If he looked good, we would be moving to the other side of the street, where I noticed a very elegant wine bar. I was aware I was not dressed for a wine bar, but it was Renton, and it was five on Friday, so I believed it would be fine. I was wearing a pair of ragged jeans, with high boots, a black blouse with a very small cleavage. With my prominent chest I never needed cleavage to emphasize it. These were my usual thoughts when I dressed up for a date.

I watched the area closely to see Mike Jr. arrive. I needed the extra few seconds to make a quick decision about how this date was going to look. I saw an elegant black BMW, very shiny, coming down the road, speeding much more than it should for the area. The driver parked next to Top Pot and made a clean reverse parking move. I love men who know how to drive and park. It was a convertible, so everybody could hear the music coming from inside the car. R&B. Exactly the music I liked. The driver was black, handsome and…wore sunglasses. What was it with these sunglasses? It was five p.m. in March in Seattle. Sun is not something that we have around usually, and especially not at that time of year. The window went up, the roof closed, and the guy stepped out of the car. He looked to be 5' 7", chubby, and dressed in very expensive clothes. Sports/elegant, but I could see the quality and the fact that this person took the time to dress up.

I smiled while I thought all these thoughts and kept looking around me. Mike Jr. should be there any second; it was ten minutes after five. I did not like people who were late. Especially not guys on our first date.

The man, from the cool black car, with the cool music, in the great apparel walked toward me. While he walked closer, I realized it was Mike Jr. Yup, this was the Mike Jr. that I was expected to meet. His pictures online must have been from a few years earlier, as he looked different in person. He had gained weight, and his hair, which was a combination of salt and pepper was not all in place, I mean, on his head, anymore. I did like the salt and pepper that was there.

I made a quick decision to change the date location and waited for him to reach me. He walked very slow, looked around him, straightened his clothes, looked like he had all the time in the world.

It was 5:15 p.m. When Mike Jr. reached me, he did not hesitate for a minute. He stopped, grabbed me, and hugged me, and his first words were, "Hi, baby." It all happened so fast. I was not ready. However, he smelled good, and his hug was not too long, although it was too close for a first hug. Oh well, he was checking the merchandise. He was strong, although chubby, and made every effort to show me and the world his manhood.

"Nice to meet you, Mike Jr." I finally got the chance to get out of his hug and looked at his face. His sunglasses were still on, so I stared at his nose, as I couldn't look into his eyes. I felt distanced, like in the army when you've just joined, and you are nobody. Remember, I served in the IDF, so I know what I'm talking about. I wondered when he would take the sunglasses off. It was now dark, and it looked weird. Okay, it looked stupid.

He had a very deep voice, and I became addicted to it right away. I suggested we move our date across the street. Mike Jr. looked toward the place I pointed. He could not see much, because of his sunglasses. He pushed the glasses a little down his nose, so he could glance over the frames. I still could not see his eyes. Okay, he said and grabbed me by my waist like he had been doing it forever. I let him. We had about fifty feet to get to the wine bar, and I did not want to waste time on arguments right now. I wanted to sit and have a glass of wine first.

The place was gorgeous. A complete surprise. Huge chandeliers hung down low from high ceilings. A little toward the dark side. Space looked rustic and rich at the same time. The place was half full. Most of the crowd consisted of white women in groups. It looked like it was a happy hour time, and some girlfriends were taking advantage of it. The prices were fifty percent discounted for the next hour, and when you are on a budget, it makes a huge difference. I loved girlfriends who go out together for a happy hour date. They usually let themselves drink a little too much, order lots of food, and enjoy it together. I knew how it worked—been there done that. We could hear the laughter from different tables around us. The atmosphere was all about fun and wine. The place had a delicious smell in the air, gentle and yummy, perhaps garlic bread, and I was hungry right away. I knew I had made a decision to not eat anything, but hey, that was true for the donut, not for here.

There were a few other men there, but Mike Jr. was the only black person in the wine bar. He did his "over the frame" glance again and looked around. I thought I saw him memorizing every detail. On the other hand, I was not sure what exactly was he doing, as the place was dark, and I still could not see how his face looked all together in one piece without sunglasses. It started to annoy me.

The waitress arrived with the menus and some water. Mike Jr. finally took his sunglasses off. The place was dark, and he could not read the menu. Hallelujah. Yes, we had a problem, Houston. Alternatively, at least, Mike Jr. thought he had a problem. One of his eyes was completely off at a weird angle. *So, this was your story, Mr. Distance.* This was what you tried to hide? Well, I had to admit that I didn't care. I always held the opinion that it is not about how you look but who you are. I was all ears and wanted to know the man behind the sunglasses. We enjoyed small talk about the weather and traffic, very polite, and read from the happy hour menu.

I saw Mike Jr. examining me, up and down, very closely. Suddenly he got his head very close to my head and whispered to my ear, "Have you ever dated a black man?"

I have to admit that it took me by surprise. Already? It had been ten minutes since we had met. I held myself together, so I wouldn't start laughing.

I did not lose my "cool Renata" spirit, and at that moment, I decided that every black guy, who ever asked me again if I had ever dated a black man, would receive the answer, "No. You are the first one. You are the first black man I have ever sat down with, had coffee/wine/drink, and have ever considered for a romantic encounter. I am a 'Black Man' virgin."

Now came my turn, and I got closer to Mike's ear, and whispered: "Never. *You* are my first and only." Goddam Improve classes. It was in my blood.

Mike Jr. loved my answer, and I saw how his whole posture changed to relaxed and happy. It was like he just got a puppy and now enjoyed its softness. I felt like the puppy, as two seconds later his hand was on my knee. Then on my thighs, trying to get me closer to him, and moving my chair, or rather, high bar stool. I did not like it and felt unsafe. When I removed his hand from there, he went to my waist. At this point, I jumped down from my stool—I am small, so I had to jump—took it and moved it to the other side of the table. Away from him. Mike Jr. put his sunglasses back on in no time and raised his distance wall again. Oh well, maybe it would not be such a pleasant date as I had thought, after all.

Mike Jr. started talking, with his deep manly voice, and the subject was his business. He had a PR firm, and he was very proud of it. He was a one-man organization, and everything was about him being black and providing PR services for black politicians and black businesses.

Mike Jr. had an eighteen-year-old daughter; she was beautiful—he shared her picture with me. He was looking for a real relationship. *Already*? We just met. He told me the woman who agreed to be his wife (!) would have a great life, but she also would have to be part of his company and support him there. He had been divorced for the past nine years.

I was very happy to see our order arrive. Mike Jr.—without asking me—ordered us a wine-tasting treat, which meant four different samples of wine, for each one of us, and a small plate of antipasto cold cuts with some cheese. It was perfect. Mike Jr. also stopped talking for few minutes, which was not bad at all. I was tired hearing about how great he was and about the requirements list he had in place for his future partner.

Mike Jr. had lived in Renton for many years and had been divorced for nine years. He said he was ready for something new. He showered me pictures of him with local celebrities. Unfortunately, I did not recognize anybody. I was not familiar with the local politics or the PR world. I just kept nodding and hummed, while he kept flashing pictures on his cell phone in front of my chewing mouth. Nothing would stop him or me.

The only thing Mike Jr. asked me, personally, was where I worked and in what position. Me, on the other hand by the end of the discussion, learned that Mike Jr. came from a very high-ranking aristocratic black family, and that he had three different names, between his first name and his last name—Mike Redford the second, Jr., Simpson. I loved it! I thought that this was hilarious. Mike Jr. gave me his business card, and his name just took over the whole card. With a last name like mine, I appreciate anybody who had a longer one. In Mike Jr.'s case, he made it his pride.

We finished the wine and the food in about an hour, while darkness took over the city outside. The lights were soft and warm in the wine bar, and I was a little tipsy. It was time to say goodbye. Mike Jr. insisted on paying the bill after he took it in his hands and looked at it. Twenty-six dollars. He hummed to himself and then made the offer. "Thank you," I said. He then held my hand, brought it to his lips and kissed it. I love these gestures. I melted a little.

Mike Jr. took the effort and walked me to my car. I had a new Ford C-Max, an electric car, and I knew he would be impressed.

We crossed the street, and he grabbed me very hard and held me next to his body. We were three hundred feet from my car; I did not say much. He was strong and smelled good, so it was not all bad, and my car was just there.

Mike Jr. let me go when I opened the driver's door and tried to get into my car. But not for long. He then grabbed me again, and this time he kissed me, a huge long French kiss. He caught me by surprise. It took me few good seconds to push him off, and it was enough for him to give me a big smile.

There was something weird or even vicious in his smile, but it was dark, I was tipsy, and it was not the time to analyze it.

"Would you like to come to my place for a dinner I will cook for you?" he asked.

"Sure. I would love to have a taste of your cooking," was my reply. I was surprised, he did not give me the impression, until then, of a guy who would cook for his loved one, a woman. More of a guy who expected that *his woman* would cook for him. I could be wrong; I remembered thinking while driving home. I shouldn't judge so quickly. Maybe he was a cool guy and was just nervous and was trying to impress me. I believed in second chances, and in my old age, I did not believe in love at first sight. It was my turn to walk the walk. I would go for dinner at his place, and I would bring something that I had made from scratch. I was sure he would appreciate it.

When I got home, I already had two text messages from Mike Jr., thanking me for a wonderful date and reminding me, that in two days he was cooking dinner for me at his place. Well, he already had a date and time. He had not even asked me if I was free. I checked my calendar, and surprise—I was free and confirmed with him our date. The only text I received after that was his address, and the time he expected me to arrive. In the two days until our date, he hadn't bothered to get in touch with me. Was he playing hard to get?

I was very curious and had many thoughts about the date, while I got ready for it. I usually had a rule not to visit a guy's place, unless I have dated him a few times already, or I just want to spend few hours with him in bed. In this case, both rules were not in place. In this case, it was his place I was curious to see, and his art choices hanging on the walls. How this place looked after nine years as a divorced man. He had not referred to any relationships since then, in our "long" first discussion, but he did mention, more than once, that he had decorated his place—by himself.

Mike Jr. talked a lot about how much work and love he had put into the place, and how he had made it cozy and relaxing. Oh, and I wanted to see a black guy's place. Would it be different? I didn't know. I just wanted to see.

During our date, Mike Jr. mentioned more than once his deck from where he could see Mount Rainer. This completely got me. I loved to see Mount Rainer from different angles in Seattle, and Renton was a new spot. It also meant I couldn't smoke there. Mike Jr. didn't smoke, but he mentioned the fact that he had dated smoking women before, and he had no problem with it. I mentioned that I also smoked weed, and he said it was okay, as long as I didn't smoke inside the house. Deal.

Two days went by quickly, and I was getting dressed to go to Mike Jr.'s place. I was supposed to arrive around five so we could still have some light to see the mountain. Yup, Mount Rainer was part of my goal list.

I could not decide what to wear. Mike Jr. hadn't texted me for the past couple of days, and I didn't try to text him, either. It felt like a game—he had gotten me to come to his place, so he didn't need to do anything more. I was coming to him. I had this gut feeling that it was not okay, but it was too late to cancel, as he must have prepared everything already, right? These were very quick thoughts that ran through my mind. It was a long drive to his place, and I hurried. I needed to leave if I wanted to be there on time. I took with me a bottle of red wine and some homemade hummus—my specialty and to-die-for dish. Authentic and made from scratch and with much love. I noticed that many people in the west coast area are familiar and love hummus, and I was sure Mike Jr. would be very happy and appreciative with this gesture.

I chose a black blouse, buttoned, and decided not to unbutton it, as I would in a different situation. The buttons stay buttoned almost to the top, but it still looked good. I decided to wear these ugly Lama Wool socks that I had bought a couple of years ago. They are soft and cozy, and I love them. I did mention ugly, right? However, I didn't really care. If I needed to take off my shoes, these would work well. High black boots and blue jeans completed the outfit, and off I went.

My silhouette will always be very noticeable. Let's say that I can compete with a few women in this world, and one of them is Dolly Parton, the other one is Pamela Anderson. I had lost much weight lately, again, and I looked very sexy. I felt great, and it was all over me. Tina said I had the Mojo.

Mojo it is! I sang to myself and kicked myself out of the house. I texted Tina the name of the guy and his address and let her know that I would be home before midnight. A routine that we had established between us, to be safe and just in case.

It was Sunday, and it was a working day the next morning. The drive to Mike Jr. 's place was forty-five minutes from my house. To remind you, I still lived in the boonies.

When I was very close to Mike Jr.'s place, about a third of a mile according to the GPS, I was lost. The GPS had lost connection, and I could not find the street that I had written down as his address. I called him, but before I had a chance to say a word, he said, "You were supposed to be here six minutes ago." Wow, a guy that likes to be on time. I could relate to that, especially after he was fifteen minutes late to our first date.

"Sorry, I am a little lost," I apologized, "but I am close to you." Mike Jr. could not understand how I was lost, as he had given me an exact address. I explained that the GPS had lost connection, and maybe if I told him which street I was on he could guide me from there while on the speaker.

Mike Jr. was not happy, and he raised his voice a little. My gut feeling became a stomach ache. It did not feel good. I stopped the car on the corner of a street that I recognized as having already passed at least once. I was driving in circles.

"I am on the corner of Fifth and Maple Avenue south. I am parking right now. Am I far from you? Do you want to help me from here, as my GPS just died?"

I heard some air blowing out on the other side, and then silence. I guessed I lost him while I was talking. "Hello, are you still there?"

"Yes, I am," Mike Jr. said and explained to me quickly that his street was in a weird corner at the next right, and I should take a sharp right to get there. Then he hung up. At least the line was dead. I wanted to think that we just lost connection.

It was a very sharp right turn, and I would not have found it if it was not for his last instructions. It was a little up the hill, on a very small street. Mike Jr.'s house was on top of the hill. An old house, and from the outside, it did not appear to be very well maintained. However, the view! I just had to get out of my car and raise my head up. I could see, between the houses, Mount Rainier. It was a bright, crisp day, and the sun was going down. It was just amazing. I took a big breath, and a wide smile spread across my face.

I made sure to take the goodies with me and marched toward the entrance. I always marched; I never just walked. I think it is because I am a petite woman in a world of tall people. I had to keep the pace.

I climbed ten old loose stairs and knocked on the door. I hoped to see Mike Jr. waiting outside, making sure I arrived safely, but there was no sign of him. Five minutes passed, and I was still outside waiting for the door to open. The sun was going down now, and it was not so crisp anymore. A little chilly to stand outside, as I had not worn a coat. I heard noise from inside, so I knocked on the door again. Footsteps approached. Somebody was walking fast, the door suddenly opened wide, and Mike Jr. was standing there, with a phone next to his ear talking very loud. He nodded for me to come inside.

I walked in quietly, feeling I was in the wrong place at the wrong time. However, I was there. Mike Jr. slammed the door, locked it in three different places, and walked away, while he was on the phone talking all the time. He suddenly stopped, and ordered me, using his hands as signals, to take off my boots. He then turned around and walked away. He did not wait for me. I took off my boots, unzipping each one of these long boots took a while, and I blessed myself for putting on the thick socks and followed his route. Three steps up inside the house, to a very large rustic kitchen. It was all there, but it was all old and not so clean, either. Mike Jr. still had the phone attached to his ear. He walked around and was looking for something. He found it. It was a Bluetooth that went in his ear very quickly. Now he could put the phone down while he kept talking. All this time, there was no head nod or a smile from his side toward me to recognize my presence. I assumed this was an important call, so I grabbed a chair next to the kitchen table and sat. The kitchen table was full of newspapers, mail, and other papers. It looked more like an office working table than a kitchen table.

I saw a lovely piece of salmon on the counter, with an olive oil bottle and fresh garlic next to it. I smiled. He was not the first guy who invited me over for dinner and prepared a salmon. Preparing a salmon was one of the easiest dishes in the world that I became familiar with since moving to the West coast. It was always a sure success, without putting in too much effort or risk. It was usually accompanied, at this time of the year, with fresh asparagus and small potatoes.

Bingo! I was so damn good; a huge smile was all over my face. I saw a bunch of fresh asparagus and a bowl with small potatoes. Mike Jr. looked at me, and suddenly walked and stood in the middle of my lookout. He blocked my view to the kitchen. I took a long look at him. He wore one stripe home sandals—I hated them on both women and men, but even more on men—sports' shorts—very short and not flattering to his crooked legs—and a white buttoned dress shirt, which ultimately did not go with all the rest he was wearing. Hmmm, it was a white shirt, and he was about to cook. This was going to be interesting. I, personally, never had had any white blouses, as I would get them dirty in thirty seconds from the minute I put it on. Especially the front part of my body.

Mike Jr. was still on the phone, but his hands were free now, and he used them to block my viewpoint. He turned around and went to the sink and started moving the products that were next to it. I finally heard him saying: "Okay, honey, let me know if you need any more help. I am here to help you with anything you need."

Oh... how sweet, I thought, NOT. Who the fuck was he talking to in front of me, and did it mean that he was going to run to his phone every time it rang? I guessed he would, as he left the Bluetooth device on his ear after he finished the call.

Mike Jr. finally looked at me and smiled. He asked me if I knew who was on the phone.

"Not at all," I said, as I really hadn't heard anything, until his last sentence. I was just not listening and was more into looking around, I guess. I liked to look at rooms and examine the different pictures on the walls when I walk into new places. In Mike Jr.'s case, I could see the living room from the kitchen and a huge wall that was all glass that could be opened up to the beautiful view in the outside. This was the deck that Mike Jr. had mentioned, and YES! I saw Mount Rainier, and although the sun was already halfway down, the view was still apparent.

He told me his daughter had been on the phone, eighteen-year-old Jennifer. Jennifer was looking at colleges, and Mike Jr. had helped her write the applications to the different colleges and reviewed every application she sent. That evening she had a meeting with a professor, who happened to be in town, from one of the colleges where she had applied. The interview was with a black woman professor, and Mike Jr. knew somebody who knew somebody who knew the professor. He now needed to call this somebody to get some more details. I would have to excuse him, but this was important.

"Of course," I said. "Do you mind if I go out to the deck and smoke there, while you are on the phone?

Mike Jr. approved the plan and was already dialing this somebody. I now had to go and find my boots and put them back before I could walk out, as Mike Jr. asked me to take them off when I had arrived. Not sure why he asked it, as the carpet looked old and tattered, but of course, I followed and respected his request.

Mike Jr. was very loud on the phone, using a strong voice and strong words. He laughed a little and talked a lot. I opened the deck's sliding glass door, anxious to go outside. It was beautiful just to stand there. I could see Mount Rainier from every corner of the deck, and while the sun kept going down, I felt that the air around me changed as well. Everything became sweeter. I wasn't sure if it was from the joint I had just lit, or if there was something in the air in a place that was so high, but it was a magical moment. There were no chairs or tables on the deck, and I found an old pot to use as an ashtray. I would pick it up later, I promised myself. At that moment, I was all enchanted with the colors that were changing just in front of my eyes, while Mount Rainer looked like somebody had just splashed it in rainbow colors.

I finished my smoke and walked back inside. I took off my boots and made sure I was doing everything as quietly as possible, as Mike Jr. was still on the phone. I sat next to the messy kitchen table and tried not to listen to his conversation, which was very hard, as the place was not big, and I had nothing to do but play with my phone. There was no Wi-Fi, so I couldn't even do that.

It took another fifteen minutes for him to finish his call. When he ended the call, he shouted his words at me, to let me know he needed to call his daughter next.

"I'll wait on the deck," I told him, "it's really nice out there right now." Mike Jr. did not even raise his eyes, and was already on the next call, talking with his daughter.

Here I go again. I put on my boots, rolled a joint and walked out.

This time I sat on the deck's floor, with the pot next to me and my back leaning on the house's wall. It was quiet outside, and the neighbors' houses were very close. I noticed all decks could watch each other; privacy was not taken into consideration when these houses were built. But nothing mattered, and I closed my eyes, just letting myself enjoy the quiet. I felt the last few sun rays touching my face, and I inhaled in all the smoke I could get from the last deep puff I took. I just finished another joint. Life was good. This was a view and a moment to die for.

I suddenly heard hard knocking on the glass door. Mike Jr. stood there, banging on the other side of the glass door to get my attention, and he did not look very happy. I got up, and the door was opened by him. I walked inside.

"Take off your boots," he ordered me with his loud voice. It almost sounded like "take off your clothes."

I smiled and assured him that I was on it. Mike Jr. did not bother closing the door, and instead turned around and went back to the kitchen.

I closed the glass door, gave my last glance to Mount Rainier, and followed him back to the kitchen. "Can I help with something?" I asked and realized that I had not had a chance to show Mike Jr. what I had brought with me. I turned and went back to the entrance and looked for the stuff. It took me a minute to get oriented, as the door was on the side of the wall and not in the middle, like in every normal place. I left my stuff behind when I walked in and I had to take off my boots—for the first time.

"Where are you going?" It sounded like Mike Jr. was almost yelling at me.

"I brought something for you," I answered from the entrance door and grabbed the hummus and the wine. It was a bottle of Merlot, which I was introduced to few months ago, and totally fell in love with it.

I brought my offerings to Mike Jr. in the kitchen. When he saw the wine, he was not impressed at all and placed it aside. As for the hummus, he opened his refrigerator and showed me a huge hummus container he had bought at the store the other day. But this is homemade hummus, I told him with a smile. Made by an authentic Middle Eastern woman. Again, Mike Jr. was not impressed.

"Here, you just have to try it," I said. I saw some mini carrots in a bag behind him and tried to reach for it. But Mike Jr. blocked me. Again.

"What are you doing?" he asked me.

"I just wanted you to try the hummus with a piece of a carrot. If you like hummus you are going to love this one," I promised him. He was not interested and said we could try it later, when he finished preparing dinner. Yes, nothing had been made yet, the fish and all the veggies were still on the table as they were when I walked in forty minutes earlier. Nothing had changed on that side of the world.

Mike Jr. asked me to go back to where I was before and sit next to the kitchen table. He poured me a glass of Shiraz and was very proud of the wine. I then enjoyed his lecture about the grapes, the taste, and the price. He was a wine snob and was very proud of it. I hated snobs; it did not matter in which field, so I got a little troubled, but then I tasted the wine, and I had to admit that it was fantastic. Mike Jr. was very proud of himself and made a point to tell me that I should never argue with him, as he is always right. I started to laugh—a black guy is talking like a Polish Jewish woman—but I stopped very quickly when he looked confused and hostile.

"Oh, you just sounded like a Polish woman,' I said. "I am always right, including the times that I am wrong." I tried to explain the joke to him, but Mike Jr. had no idea what I was talking about. He was not familiar with jokes about Polish Jewish women and had no interest to hear or understand them. Oh well, I took a sip of the wine, maybe I would just get tipsy a little while he made dinner, as I felt my stomach starting to talk. It had been a few hours since the last time I had eaten. And I'd had two joints and no water. The wine hit me very quickly, and I felt just fine.

Mike Jr. talked about his work, and how important it was for the black community and the world. He was the only black person who had his own PR company in the area, and he worked with all the black politicians in town. He was involved in few boards that supported black women and kids to provide more education. They had grants and funds and had a significant gala fundraising coming in a couple of weeks. It was a black-tie event, and if things were serious between us, he might invite me to go with him.

Oh, really, how nice of you. Not really my cup of tea, but you keep talking, I thought. I decided to enjoy my glass of wine. I watched him cutting and again offered my help.

Maybe by setting the table? Mike Jr. finally agreed and asked me to take the pile of things that were on the table and move them to the table in the living room. There was a pile of papers there as well, so I made sure to move it a little, to make a place for the new pile of papers I brought with me.

"Don't move anything on the table," I heard him shouting from the kitchen. He saw what I was doing. Oh well, too late. I left the papers there while going back to the kitchen. As the kitchen was raised up three steps from the living room, I could sit there and see the view outside, but it was only half of a view now because of the darkness.

The table was cleared, but not so clean. I asked Mike Jr. for a piece of cloth to clean the table, and he just moved me from his way, went to the table, and cleaned it. He swiped the dirt into his hands, while the majority of it fell on the floor.

"Here, clean," he said.

Yes, completely clean. I set the table with dishes that he provided, the napkins were improvised from paper towels, which I did my best to fold in a really nice elegant way. My Polish heritage was in control every time it came to setting the table.

Mike Jr. was not impressed and did not say a word. He chopped veggies and threw them into the sizzling pan. He was a big guy, so his back was now taking over the corner where he worked. The phone rang again. It was his daughter on the line, and she needed him to look at something right away and give his opinion. It was almost seven o'clock, and I had arrived there at 5:30. Dinner would not be served very quickly. Well hell, it was not even going to be cooked soon. Fish is quick to cook, I reminded myself and took another sip of my wine.

The discussion was getting very hectic. I heard Mike Jr. explaining to his daughter how to answer different questions, and she just faxed him her updated resume. I could hear the fax machine beeping, while he ran toward it.

I took my wine and made my way to the deck, after putting my boots on. Again. I tried to catch Mike Jr.'s attention/eyes for a sec to let him know I was going out, but he was busy and ignored me. I decided not to bother him. This sounded like it would be a long call.

I rolled myself another joint and again sat on the floor, with my back on the wall and the pot/ashtray next to me. It really felt comfortable now, primarily when the glass of wine was just next to me. Excellent wine, I thought and took another sip, while blowing away some smoke. It was almost entirely dark, and the shadows were running all over the place playing hide and seek. Just a quiet picturesque moment in a peaceful place.

And then I heard banging on the glass door, and Mike Jr. stood there waving his hands all over the place. He held some papers and signaled me to come inside. Sigh. A quick look at my watch showed that I had been outside for almost twenty minutes. Back in, it is, so I walked in, took off my boots, again, and walked to the kitchen. I was, again, happy and thankful for the fact I brought my warm ugly Lama socks. They were well padded, and the floor was tough and bumpy in few places. As I had a toe surgery not long time ago, I found it hard to walk without shoes, unless it was a sandy beach. Good luck with this in Seattle.

Mike Jr. was very busy in the kitchen, and I heard him putting things into the oven and chopping very loudly. I sat down next to the kitchen table, again, and watched him. He was talking to me and describing his daughter's resume and how he helped her upgrade it just now. I asked Mike Jr. when dinner would be ready, thinking about some more wine. Mike Jr. turned around sharply, walked toward me, with a big spatula in his hand, and waved it very angrily in front of my face. He was upset that I had gone out to smoke so many times, and that I smoked weed on his deck. I apologized, reminded him that I had told him in advance that I smoked, and that marijuana was my poison. I mentioned very calmly that he had been busy on the phone for a long time, and I wanted to respect his privacy. He gave me an annoyed look, and then lectured me, for a whole five minutes, about how busy he was and that the woman in his life should accept it and wait for him when he was dealing with his business. "Do you understand that?" he asked me. "Do you understand that there will be times that I will have to talk to people and work my business, while you will be waiting until I'm done? My woman needs to respect and support me every second. I want a woman who knows how to wait quietly."

Well, Houston, we have a problem. Mike Jr. did not wait for an answer and went back to finish his cooking mission. I took the wine bottle, poured some for myself and took it over to fill his glass. He handed me his glass for a refill, and we both said cheers while launching our drinks. He said "Cheers," and I said "Le'Hayim." Mike Jr. looked at me confused, and I explained to him that this is the Jewish term for cheers, and it means "For Life." No comment came from his side. He suddenly turned around, grabbed me strongly, pushed me toward the refrigerator, and kissed me a long, strong kiss. Surprised, tipsy, and high, I let him do it for a long time and then pushed him slowly away. It was more than enough for me, for that moment in time.

Mike Jr. let me go and continued with his cooking as if nothing had happened. The phone rang again. He did not hesitate for a second and put his Bluetooth on—it is there all the time, just next to him on the counter. His daughter was on the line, again. Jennifer was not sure what to wear and was now discussing it with her father. He didn't say a word about having a guest over, and I'm sure she thought she had her father all to herself alone in his house. I wondered if she would have called so many times if she had known her father had a woman over for dinner.

This time I did not leave the table, and I listened to the discussion that was very hysterical from Jennifer's side. Mike Jr. kept calling her "my baby, my sweet honey, baby girl," and so on. Mike Jr. was firm but also very gentle with Jennifer and gave her some excellent advice, from what I could hear. When he finally finished the call with Jennifer, I knew exactly what clothes she would be wearing—black skirt and a white shirt—what shoes—a black high heel—and how she was doing her hair—letting it down, after she has straightened it. Mike told her to wear minimal jewelry, and the impression I got was of some charming young, professional woman. It was a beautiful picture that I had in my head of Jennifer. Good luck to her, I whispered quietly, but Mike Jr. did not hear me. He was still giving last minute advice.

Eventually, the food was ready—oven timer went off—and luckily Mike Jr. ended his call. Good luck to your daughter, I told him when he came with the plates to the table.

"Oh, she will be just fine. She does not know it, but she is in. My friend assured me he will talk to the professor, who he knows personally." But, of course, this is how it worked when you have a father who has a PR agency and knows all the politicians in town.

Finally, we started eating. Mike Jr. baked a fresh, beautiful, amazing piece of salmon wrapped in a foil paper with lemon and herbs. Small potatoes and asparagus accompanied it. Charming dinner, and I was happy to have it. It took almost two hours to get to this moment, but every bite was delicious. I took another sip of wine, and...just dug into the food, starving. The hummus was not anywhere in the picture.

I needed this food. I felt my head spinning, and my stomach started to hurt, crying for help and screaming "feed me." At this point, I had had four glasses of wine—

Mike Jr. did open the wine I brought and did agree that it was not bad—and three loaded joints. When I drink and smoke, I have my libido increased. What a fun fact, isn't it?

Suddenly, Mike Jr. grabbed my chair and drew it very close to him. Although I had lost a lot of weight, I will never be a skinny woman, so he had to put a lot of strength into it, and he continued with his moves. He whispered something in my ear. I could not understand what he said, but I smiled, which was a big mistake. He grabbed me in his arms and walked me into the other part of the house. He took me to his bedroom.

The bedroom was huge, with a ninety-inch TV screen that was turned on and broadcasting a basketball game. The bed was enormous, king, of course. Mike Jr. threw me on the bed. I found myself without my shirt and bra, and Mike Jr. trying to take off my pants. He managed to take off my socks and aimed for my pants. I asked him if he had a condom, but he ignored me. It all happened so fast, that only at this point I stopped him, and asked him to relax and go slowly. His face got red, and he barked at me, "I do not sleep around, but it looks like you do." Reminder, we just met a couple of days ago, through an online dating site.

Mike Jr. suddenly took both my boobs and just slammed them together. OUCH! This hurt, and I woke up from my sweet buzz right on the spot. I pushed him away from me—hard— and sat down on the bed. "What is wrong with you?" I asked him. Mike Jr. did not answer, and just lay down on the bed and began watching the TV screen. He completely ignored me as if I was not there and nothing had happened.

I got off the bed, picked up my stuff, put on my clothes, but I could not find one of my Lama socks. I was not going to spend any more time looking for it. I needed to get out of there immediately. I put on one sock and left the room. Mike Jr. was still lying on the bed watching TV.

I got my purse and put on my boots. Again. It was cold without one sock. The kitchen looked like a war had just occurred. The sink area was all dirty, full of leftovers from Mike Jr.'s preparations, and the kitchen table was all messed up. When Mike Jr. had picked me up in his arms, it had been pushed hard and everything that was on the table got slammed. The wine bottle was dripping on the floor. I didn't care. I needed to get out of there right away.

When I tried to open the front door, I found out that I could not. It was locked in a way that I could not figure out. I noticed that there was another door, half a floor down, and I tried that exit as well. Still I couldn't get out. I went back to the main entrance, where I thought I had entered when I arrived. I tried to figure out how to open it.

Mike Jr. was suddenly next to me. "What are you doing?" he asked me.

"I'm getting out of here as quickly as I can," I answered him, still fighting with the door. He pressed a secret button on top of the door, and the door opened. I did not wait for a second more, and was out of his house, walking—almost running so fast that I could hardly breathe.

I got into my car and was shaking. I started the car and tried to control my shaking so I could drive safely. I got to the corner of the street and had to park. My heart was running so fast, that I felt I had no air in my chest—and I have a big one. What had happened? I tried to run the past ten minutes in my mind, to understand, and it did not help. I needed to relax and get my breath back. It was hard, and I felt I was shaking even more. It took me ten more minutes to calm down. I tried to concentrate on my breathing and control my heart beats. It slowly went down. And then I remembered again how he slammed my breast, and my heart started racing like crazy. I felt fear, humiliation, and…lucky. Lucky that I had gotten myself out of there and nothing worse had happened.

I got home and texted Tina that I had arrived. It was still early in the evening, 9:30. Tina replied, asking about the date, as it was early in the evening, and I usually take my time.

I called Tina and told her what had happened. She was shocked. I was as well. Still shocked. Mike Jr. was a dangerous man, and I was lucky to get out of there with no harm.

"But what about your sock?" she asked, and we both started laughing. I needed this laugh…it cleansed me, and I felt much better after sharing the events with Tina.

"It was stupid of me to trust him and go to his house," I told her. His business card and stories made an impression of a professional man, and I ignored all the red lights because of this impression. It was a hard-core lesson to learn about the dangers of dating.

Mike Jr. sent me a text message the next day to tell me he had found my sock, and he could send it to me if I gave him an address. Not a home address of course, but he could send it to my office if I wanted it. I replied by telling him, that he could use the sock instead of a condom next time he was missing one, and I blocked his number.

This experience made my "go black" plan go "on hold" for a long time. I knew there were assholes out there, and it didn't matter what color they were. But, Mike Jr. played the black card so hard, that I decided that I needed a break from the plan. I didn't date or even enter into an online discussion with a black guy, for many months after this experience.

5 - HOW THICK IS YOUR DICK?

When I separated from my husband and decided to open an online dating account, I was immediately bombarded with men's messages, which boosted my confidence and made me feel amazing about myself. I remember a very special phone conversation I had with a guy, who I will name Four-inch Mike. He had this amazing sexy voice, a voice you would die for, or at least, do anything he asked you to do. Deep manly voices are one of my soft spots. Four-inch Mike asked me out for dinner on Friday at a place called "New Horizons." I agreed and Googled the place after we finished the call.

I discovered that New Horizons was a swingers' club. The guy wanted to take me, on our first date, to a swingers' club. Although I was curious to visit a place like that, I felt tricked and was very upset. Four-inch Mike had not asked me for dinner, he had asked me to have sex. I texted him right away, thanked him, but no thank you, Four-inch Mike, this was not my thing, and have a good life.

Four-inch Mike called me right away, and started, with his deep, sexy amazing to-die-for voice to convince me. "Renata, it's a private club, they have a private chef. You don't have to do anything you don't want to do."

"Oh really? Thank you, but no thank you," I repeated and ended the call.

A week later, I was on a date with a really cute short Asian guy, and we had a great three-hour first date. We decided to continue to a bar near my place, and he followed my car there. On the way, I changed my mind about the location, and I touched my phone to dial his number. When I heard the call answered, I shouted with my very not soft voice, "So, I changed my mind, and we are going to…" Before I could finish, I heard this amazing, deep sexy voice on my phone.

"Good evening, Renata. I knew you would call again." Yes. I had dialed Four-inch Mike's number by mistake.

It was eleven at night, and I apologized. "Mike, I'm sorry for the late hour. I really apologize, but I dialed your number by mistake." It sounded as if Four-inch Mike hadn't heard me because he continued talking.

"Renata, do you want to know how thick my dick is?"

I almost had an accident at that moment. Lucky me, the road was clear as it was late in the evening, and we were out of the city on a side road. I wondered what the Asian guy who followed me thought about my driving skills at that point.

"Mike, I'm in the middle of a date with a 6' 6" black guy. Do you really think your dick is thicker than his?"

I heard silence on the line. I really felt bad for Four-inch Mike. "Okay, okay, Mike, please tell me how thick your dick is."

"Four," he said.

"Inches?" I asked. He assured me I had heard him correctly. I needed to calculate it for a second in my European head, and then I asked, "Is that diameter or circumference?"

I heard a click in my ear. Needless to say, he never called me again.

6 - YOUNG DOLLY PARTON

There were many things I learned as a new divorcee. When I first met my ex-husband, he had just turned nineteen, and I was fourteen and a half years old—a very mature fourteen, or at least I looked older, thanks to my substantial big front.

I have had big boobies since the age of thirteen. I realized very early on in my development that my life would change because of them. I remember coming back home one day from the beach—a ten-minute walk from my parents' condo—crying and pissed-off like crazy. I was almost fourteen at that time.

My mother, who had big boobies herself—I had to inherit it from somebody—was trying to understand what had happened, and there was no way I could get her off my back.

My dear Polish mom, who knitted and crocheted tablecloths, sweaters, and many other things, decided over the previous winter to crochet me a swimming suit. A bikini one. She saw it in a magazine from Paris. My mom chose a color that was almost my skin color, so when I wore it, it looked as if I was naked.

When my mom measured me at home during the winter, the bra piece kept changing size, so she kept adding "lines" to it. The only "not-skin color" on my bikini was a black line around the bra piece and around the bikini bottom. To add to it, in the middle of the lower piece, right on the holy triangle, she added a small flower. Very artistic, you might think, but again, from far away it looked a little different.

Our condo was on the fourth floor with no elevator, so I made a point not to forget anything when I left. It was also a ten-minute walk to the beach. So was my middle school-high school. But from school, the beach was only a five-minute walk to the public beach. When we sat in the classrooms, we could poke our heads out of the windows and see the beach and the flag at the life guard's tower indicating the condition of the water for that day.

I used to go to the beach every day. I knew about an abandoned area of the beach with private dunes where I could hide and read. I sometimes spotted somebody I knew walking on the beach and carrying the equipment for playing matkot—the local sport on the beach, which involves two small rackets and a very small stiff ball. It requires hitting the ball hard and very precisely. If you miss a ball, and it hits you, it hurts like hell. The game also involved a lot of jumping, and if you were a suicidal person, like me, you could find yourself running to the water to save a ball and crashing into the waves.

Although I was young, I managed to play a few games with the older guys, as I was in great shape and a runner. I was just starting my feminine development in those days.

Until that fateful day, when I wore my new bikini for the first time.

When I came home from school on that particular day, I could not find my old swimming suit, and I had to run out before my mother came in and grounded me. She always grounded me for something when I was about to go out. This time, I was determined she would not catch me, so I hurriedly took the bikini that had been lying there for few days waiting for me to take it over. All the fittings were done, and it was ready to go.

I pulled a white tank top over it, and out I ran! I had just reached the bottom floor when I realized I had forgotten to take a book and a towel. I took a quick look around. There was no way I had time to make it upstairs again and still avoid my mom. She was very punctiliously precise with the time she came home and the time we arrived home. I'd told her the day before that I had a late class, so I said she wouldn't see me before four o'clock. It was 1:05 p.m., and she would be home in five minutes. I walked quickly, almost running, trying not to attract any attention from any neighbor who might see me. Everybody knew everybody there. It was a dense hood, made up of Jewish immigrants from all over the world.

I had to pass the corner curve. Once I passed it, I was out of danger, which meant my mom wouldn't see me when she was on her way home.

I made it, and I could now run to the beach. I was almost fourteen years old, and it was summer in Israel, which meant it was very hot, and the only thing I thought about was the Mediterranean Sea that I was about to plunge into very soon.

I arrived at the beach, found a small dune, and checked into it. The dunes changed every day, thanks to the wind and the weather, and it was always a challenge to find the perfect dune. There were diverse criteria to consider, such as the time of the day, where the sun was located, and how much privacy I wanted. I didn't have my book that day, so water and matkot was the best thing I could ask for.

Crazy hot in Kiryat-Yam, and it was only the beginning of the summer. June. I chose the dune closest to the water, so I could watch my stuff when I went for a swim. It was also a good spot to see all those who were walking between the beaches that are all connected to each other—2.5 miles of beaches, some of them are designated, but most of them are wild and deserted. I noticed some guys in other dunes, but they did not bother me, and I did not bother them. We were all part of the view.

Since it was a very hot day, I took my top tank off immediately and ran off to the water. Not many people were around, but I saw a couple of guys walking toward my area, and one of them was holding matkot. I knew him. He was one of the regulars on the beach and an amazing player. I never played with him before, as I was never good enough to face him. I was also a young girl, and he was in his early twenties.

Surprisingly, they walked toward me and waited for me to get out of the water. They asked for my name, and I happily shared it with them. My matkot hero asked me if I knew how to play the game. Of course, I told him. I also told him that I knew he was an amazing player, as I saw him playing before. He asked me if I wanted to try and play with him. I loved the idea and ran over to pick up one of the rackets in his hands. When I got to him, the racket fell on the sand, and he apologized, but I happily bent down, picked up the racket, and ran to the other side. Now it was me and him, and his friend sat down on the sand and watched us. I didn't put my shirt on, as I was still wet from dipping in the water.

It was an amazing game. The guy was soft on me in the beginning, but once I hit him hard with the ball, he took things seriously. I did notice that his balls were very high, and I really needed to jump high to get them. Maybe it was because I was short, and he was used to playing with taller people. Fifteen minutes later, two more guys joined and watched the game. One of them asked to join us, and suddenly, I was playing against two men in their twenties, running and jumping like crazy. Twenty more minutes, and I was done. I couldn't run or jump anymore and felt as if my skin was completely burned in the sun. I had not worn any sun screen. That was not a product that was around in my childhood.

I joined the guys who were sitting down, and they offered me some beer. It was cold, and I was happy to take a sip from it.

They were all very interested in me, and I was very happy to share my name, my age, and the school I attended. At one point, I realized it was late, and I had to leave and go home. I promised them that I would be back the next day in the same place and time. They promised to meet me for a matkot game.

When I started to leave, I saw one of the guys smiling to another guy and humming the tune from a commercial that was running in Israel back then. A very popular one. The commercial showed a bunch of girls walking on a beach, with white T-shirts and no bras. It was a very straight-forward commercial—for grapefruits. Literally an upfront one. This was what he hummed, thinking I couldn't hear him.

When I went to say goodbye to the guys who still played, I heard the same song hummed again. I started to feel very uncomfortable and made sure that all my parts were covered, and nothing was popping out.

On my walk back home, I heard the same humming from a few other men I passed, so I put my white tank top on. As I did so, I bumped into a girl friend from school. She was walking her dog and came toward me with a big smile. We hugged and said hi. Her first words were. "I was sure you were naked! Oh boy, you look naked from far away, and now you look like those girls from the grapefruits commercial."

I was so upset. Those girls were in their early twenties, and I was not even fourteen years old, and the last thing I wanted to show were my boobies.

I started to cry. Then I turned around and ran home as quickly as I could. I arrived home crying, dehydrated, and red like a lobster.

My mother heard the story and looked at my bikini. She reminded me that she still needed to sew a lining of a darker color, which would change the "skin-tone" color of its current state. And besides, she told me, one day would come when I would appreciate what I had, and I would see how many women envied me and how many men would want me.

"You just have to make sure that you are not upset and enjoy what you have," she said.

I didn't understand what she was talking about, but a new liner sounded great, and women envying me and men wanting me sounded okay as well, coming from my Polish mom. I had never heard her talk like that before. I decided to believe my mom and continue my day. In the coming weeks, I also had to leave the running team, as my chest hurt when I ran, and I could not compete with all those skinny tall girls, while I turned every day, more and more, into a curvy woman.

More than thirty years later, newly divorced, and I needed to share a picture of myself on an online dating site. Was my mother, right? Was this the time she was talking about?

All the pictures I shared on my online dating profiles had been recently taken. I decided NOT to have a picture with my "front" in it. I posted a few face pictures, and one picture, from far away, that showed a whole body, but it was hard to see details.

I had a cute face and lovely lips, so the guys had something to comment about, plus my smile was always big and full of teeth. This was how I smiled and laughed, from the bottom of my heart. I think that the men who looked at my pictures got this feeling, as most of the messages I received were nice, polite, and complimented my appearance. The messages usually started about my looks. It was rare to get a message about an interest I had listed in my profile. When I received these routine messages, I wanted to respond, "Hello, you out there. I wrote forty lines about myself in my profile, and you did not bother reading it, because my picture is so…what? Took your breath away? This is not the way to my heart."

I decided to change the strategy and play a game. I opened another account, with a new email address, on the same online dating site, OKCupid, where I'd been for a few months. My new account's nickname was "Young Dolly Parton."

The only picture seen was a picture of an ear, with three beautiful earrings on it. All studs. One could also see that the owner of this ear was blond.

When I came back from India the previous year, I brought some amazing earrings back for my daughters, and my youngest changed all her earrings to the ones I brought. The picture I shared, on Young Dolly Parton's profile, was of her ear with all the new earrings. When I posted the picture, I thought that really her ear is my ear, right? I also told her about it, and we had a good laugh together when I said that her ear belongs to me. Besides, my ear doesn't really look older, does it?

The Young Dolly Parton profile was an amazing success. I finally got in touch with men who read my profile and wrote me back based on information I provided.

The OKCupid site had a very interesting way to match you with other users. It had more than one thousand questions to answer if you wanted. OKCupid used the answers and identified the level of suitability people had between them. Answering the questions became my hobby—I would answer questions while standing in traffic—and I already answered eight hundred of them. Some of the questions were what you could call "Cosmo" questions and sounded stupid and superficial. As a project manager, a statistics graduate, and having worked with the software/algorithm world for many years, I understood the benefits behind them as well.

I remember a couple of the questions that caught my interest: Do you like beer? Do you like watching horror movies? I've found out—thank you, Google—that according to statistics, there is a correlation between all these things. In this case, if both sides like the taste of beer and watching horror movies, chances are they will have sex on their first date. I love statistics, and I believe in it, so I just kept answering questions. I love beer, and I do not like horror movies.

Back to the Young Dolly Parton profile.

I enjoyed the attention, went a step further, and took a full body picture to add to my profile. But instead of my face, I photoshopped Dolly Parton's face. So now you could see my ear, my body—but without exposing anything, but any potential dates could get the full real picture—and a profile that was very bold. Add all of this to the fact that my profile name was "Young Dolly Parton," and I got a very active online dating account, which attracted a lot of responses.

There were the responses that were "straight" and direct to their point. They wanted to know how I dared call myself Dolly! I found them boring, and I had no interest in having any discussion with them. Unfortunately, I was asked to remove this picture very quickly by OKCupid's website administrators, and I went back to the ear picture.

The interesting messages came from the men who were interested to know *why* I had posted that photo. Why had I opened an account without displaying my face, but giving a very detailed profile and a picture of an ear? These were the appealing ones. I met an ER doctor who responded to this account. We were texting each other like crazy for a week, as he was working the night shift. On the day we were supposed to meet—a Friday night—his professor at work resigned, and all his shifts moved to another doctor. This meant he was going to spend the whole weekend in the hospital. He was soooooo pissed off. I never heard a man so disappointed, pissed off and…showing his real colors. I hate people who can't control their anger and temper and use swearing to express themselves. Next please. Yes, if you are a doctor, it does not mean that you are a man of quality.

There was another guy who could not take it. He accused me of playing games, and he believed that I wasn't for real. I was fake, and this is an account the OKCupid is running. I agreed. I was playing games, and I was looking for a partner to play with me. If you couldn't handle my game now, you would not be able to handle my game later. About the fake part, I think he was referring to my boobies, and I had no desire or need to prove him wrong.

I also met a country musician who confessed to me right away that he was a Dolly admirer. I completely agreed with Mike #35 that Dolly deserved our admiration. The problem was that I knew nothing about country music, and while Dolly Parton was a fun artist for me, I was not into her music. I liked her personality, her big warm heart, and her opinions. I hoped he would find me similar to her in these areas, as he sounded really cool on the phone and in text messages. We decided to meet for a drink.

The first time we met, Mike #35 decided to take me out for dinner for Creole food. I'd spent a few months in Monroe, Louisiana, earlier in my career, so I knew a lot about the Creole cuisine and loved it.

I saw Mike #35's eyes when I walked into the restaurant. They got big…and a huge smile came with it. He was a big man at 6' 6" and carried more than few extra pounds. All of this did not stop him from getting up from his chair and giving me a big warm hug. A little too big and too warm, I felt, while he kept hugging me. I didn't say a word and let myself hug him back. It is not every day that my presence made a stranger so happy, and I just went along with it.

We had an okay time at dinner, but I did not think he would call again, as the discussion was not flying so well. Surprisingly, two days later Mike #35 did call and asked me out again. I was not very much into it, but had no plans, and dinner at the local steak house sounded great. If Mike #35 wanted to drive and pay for dinner, so be it. He was an old-school guy and refused my offer to pay half of the bill.

This time, dinner and conversation went very well. We laughed and had an amazing time for a couple of hours and found a lot of common subjects to talk about. When Mike #35 called again the next day, he said he had a show playing in Seattle at the Little Red Hen, a swing dance/music club, I was happy to accept the invite to join him.

Mike #35 played a few instruments, and at that show he was to play a banjo and a piano. We had a quick drink before the show started, and he asked me to wish him luck. I did, and he kissed me on my lips. I was not ready for that and pushed him away gently.

The Red Hen was packed. I was sitting at the bar and kept saying no to guys who asked me to dance. I had a good reason to say no. I didn't know how to swing dance! Finally, one of the guys looked at me and said,

"Just try." And I did. I loved it, and I was good! He did not believe me that it was my first swing dance. But it was. I saw Mike #35 looking at us and smiling. Then it hit me... most of the times that we would be going out, Mike #35 would be working, and I would have to dance with strangers.

I finished the dance and gave the guy my phone number. He was an amazing dancer, and I hoped he would call so I could dance with him again. He asked me to stay for a drink, I thanked him, refused, and told him that I was with one of the musicians. He disappeared almost immediately, and I did not see him for the rest of the evening.

Mike #35 had a short recess, during which he came and had a glass of water with me in the bar. During work time, he did not drink alcohol. I thanked him again for inviting me to this place, and he said that it was amazing watching me dance. I felt weird but didn't say a word. He hugged me suddenly and got my body—my boobies—very close to his chest. I was completely not ready, and he had a good minute, until I started pushing back, to get out of his hug. I tried not to be aggressive, but he was a big man and his hug was very strong this time. The MC announced that the music would continue in five minutes, which made Mike #35 stop the hug, which gave me time to breath. I told him that I would be leaving soon, as it was a "school night," and I had a long drive back to my place in the middle of nowhere. He said he would call me the next day, and we said good night.

He did call me the next day. He wanted to come over and spend some more time with me. Mike #35 lived in Olympia, and this meant he would need to stay for the night. That was not my plan, but it was his plan.

I told Mike #35 that this would not work, and he was pushing too much and too hard. He said he would call the next day. He never called again. A couple of weeks later, I saw on Facebook that he was in a relationship. I guess he was playing and dancing at more than one party at the time he was seeing me. Oh well. Dolly, here we come again.

7 - SIXTY-NINE IS NOT ALWAYS A GOOD NUMBER

The next Mike, number sixty-nine, reached out to me with a picture of himself and his dog hiking in a beautiful area around Rattlesnake Ridge in North Bend, Washington. I recognized the place right away, and he got two brownie points. One for the dog—I love dogs and have a dog as well— and one for the area—which is one of my favorites—where he chose to hike with his dog. We exchanged numbers and started texting each other almost immediately after we met online. I invited Mike #69 to visit my area with his dog, and we would meet in an off-leash dogs' park, so we could have both dogs running around and having fun, while we chatted in the open air. Since I lived in a rural area, there was plenty of open space and trees.

Mike #69's pictures showed a handsome well-built man. He was a gate designer, an artist who worked with heavy metal and built fancy gates for fancy houses. His texts were more than just "hi and bye." He really talked and shared his thoughts and feelings.

We exchanged info for days and tried to a find time to get together that worked for both of us. After a week of exchanging texts, Mike #69 wrote me that he didn't want to drive the whole way between West Seattle and the Mirrormont/Issaquah area—a forty-five-minute drive— only to be stood up.

Hmmm...this guy was hurt once and was now trying to make sure it didn't happen again. I understood and decided to be supportive. Although it did not happen to me often, I had been stood up once or twice, and I remembered how upset I was about taking the time to get ready, driving to a place we agreed on, and then just waiting for fifteen, twenty, then thirty minutes, while texting to my date and not receiving an answer back. It's very frustrating and insulting. We were all adults here, so what was the story with not arriving and suddenly disappearing? Later on, I concluded that being stood-up was a good experience, as the guy must have been an asshole to do a thing like that, so at least I wasn't stuck with him for a conversation that might not be fun or might take us to a bad place. Lemon became Limoncello.

I understood, I told Mike #69, so I offered to meet for lunch on the waterfront during the week. I would be coming from work, and we could walk around Olympic Sculpture Park and get to know each other. Mike #69 loved the idea, and we scheduled a day to meet. The location was Pier 69 on Seattle's amazing waterfront. We would choose where to have lunch while we walked around, as there were so many places that offered a great quick lunch at that time of day. Everything was settled and agreed upon.

On the day of our date, I had a really busy morning at work without a minute to sit down. It took all my attention until noon. I thought of canceling the date with Mike #69 and re-scheduling it for another day, but after his last comments about being stood-up, I didn't want him to feel rejected again, so I just grabbed my jacket at the last minute and literally ran from my office to make it on time to meet him. I estimated I would be five minutes late and texted him that fact. He answered back that he was already there waiting for me.

I had to take an elevator to the parking area, and from there take the sky bridge to get to the other side of the street to another elevator. Only people who worked in this area knew all these short cuts, and I had long felt like this was my hood, and I could find my way better than any local person from Seattle. Most of the people in Seattle were not familiar with these two elevators, which were hidden very well.

When I got to the Pier on the waterfront, I started to walk very fast, as I hated to be late to anything that I had scheduled, and I had less than an hour now to spend with Mike #69. Thanks to a day with much going on at work, I needed to get back ASAP to get things in place for an afternoon meeting.

"I should have canceled our meeting," I kept thinking. I hadn't even had a chance to look at the mirror before I left the office."

I passed a guy who sat on the stairs of one of the buildings on the waterfront, and his dog lay next to him. He sat as if he was taking a sunbath in the middle of the day. I smiled and said, "The only thing you need now is a hat, and you can also get some money for the day." He smiled back, but I was in a hurry and just continued my fast walk. It took me twenty seconds to stop walking away to realize I had just passed Pier 69. The guy I was just talking to was my date.

I felt like I was in a slow-motion movie, as my steps became slower and heavier, and I stopped to look back. Yes, I just passed Pier 69. I recognized the dog from the pictures, but the guy looked a little different than I remembered. I was almost walking backwards and had to turn around toward his direction to align myself.

"I'm sorry," I said when I got to where he sat. "I was just joking."

Mike #69 didn't say a word, but just got up from the stairs and brushed his hands on his coat.

"Nice to meet you. I'm Renata." I put my hand up for a handshake, and his dog was all over me, licking and happy to see me. We could not shake hands, as the dog was jumping on me like crazy. I guessed it smelled my dog and was therefore very friendly toward me.

We started walking and talking. Well, Mike #69 was talking. I played with the dog and tried to listen to him.

Mike #69 had moved to Seattle five months earlier from Dallas, Texas, and had his own business for designing big heavy metal gates. He saw himself as an artist. He designed the gates from scratch, including the installation, which meant he was also a certified electrician. He moved to Seattle, as he hated the weather in Dallas and wanted a change.

"What's his name?" I asked.

"Who?" he responded.

"Your dog, what is his name?"

"Oh, this is Ruby, she's been with me for six years." And he kept talking about his business, what kind of metal he used, and that he was now looking for a workshop to start a business in the Pacific Northwest. He was very proud of what he did and had been doing it for the past fifteen years. He had never married and had no children.

We kept walking. We had just passed three different places that offered food, and we were walking in a circle, starting to go back to where we met. There would be no food options there, and I felt my stomach crying for help. I knew that once I got back to the office, I would be joining a meeting right away, and it would take at least a couple of hours until I had time to grab a bite.

"She is so cute and happy," I said.

"Who?" Mike #69 asked.

"Ruby," I said, and let her jump on me and give me a big wet lick.

"Oh, she's all right. Usually she's not so hyper, but I guess she likes you." He didn't even look toward me and continued talking about his artistic gates and the mansions in Texas for which he built the gates.

We finished walking in a circle, and we were exactly in the same point where we started. We stood next to a crosswalk that would take me to the other side of the street, and to the first elevator to my office.

I bent down, took Ruby's head in my hands, and gave her a kiss and a hug. "It was nice meeting you, Ruby. You are a sweet big puppy."

The light turned to green, so I ran to catch it, as traffic, in this area is crazy, and the green light for the pedestrians is very short. I told you I'm from the hood, didn't I?

I arrived back at my office, threw my bag and jacket on my desk, and grabbed my notebook and a pen. I needed to get to a conference room on the other side of the floor. I hoped I could grab a cup of coffee from the machine, if it wasn't broken or the line too long.

I grabbed a glass of water, as the coffee machine was broken again, and walked to the meeting room. When I got there, I found out that they had changed rooms, and the new location was exactly in the opposite direction, from where I had just come.

I finally got there, just few minutes late and found out that other people were late as well, so we had to wait for them. I sat down and made small talk with those who were already in the room. But something bugged me, and I could not put my finger on it. I felt as if I had forgotten something. I checked my pocket, and my phone was there. I hadn't used my wallet, as we hadn't bought anything to eat, so it was still in my purse. What was nagging at me?

But I didn't have time to dwell on it as I had to concentrate on the meeting, as I was the main presenter and driving the conversation. I tried to push the disturbing feeling away, and I almost managed to do it when it hit me.

I hadn't said goodbye to Mike #69! I said goodbye to Ruby, gave her a kiss and a hug, and ran through the crosswalk, without even looking back.

Okay, now I could concentrate on the meeting.

I never heard from Mike #69 again. I kept looking at Pier 69 from the office window, thinking mainly about Ruby. She made a great first impression and looked like her pictures. Mike #69, on the other hand, looked older than his pictures, and I couldn't identify any mutual interest to talk about with him—unless it was his business. The number sixty-nine had not turned out to be so great this time around.

8 - MY OWN POPEYE

I was seventeen and a half and had just finished high school. Summer had started, yet I had to wait six months to be part of the IDF, the mandatory service for Israeli citizens. I could not wait to start. I wanted to serve my country, and this was part of every teenager's life after high school. It meant that you had stepped up to your adult life.

In the meantime, I worked three jobs with the first one starting at seven in the morning at the local Driving License Office. At noon, I worked in a hospital taking care of a sick kid who couldn't get out of bed, and at nights, I worked as a waitress. I worked for five days a week in a new coffee bar strategically located on the way to Carmel Mountain, which meant it had amazing views of Haifa. I loved it.

The place, which also served alcohol, had just opened and had already drawn a large crowd of regulars. A huge aircraft carrier with five thousand U.S. Navy men had landed while I worked there, and the city celebrated the white uniforms. Other new places besides the café where I worked tried to make easy and quick money as well. The city was booming. There were a lot of people looking for something to do and something to eat and drink.

The first day the coffee bar opened, I was asked to serve all the tables where the customers spoke English. I was identified as the only English speaker. I was also the only waitress there who had finished high-school. Later, I found out I was the only person in the whole place who had finished high school, including the owners and all other employees.

It was my first time to work as a waitress and my first conversation with a group of people whose first language was English. And there I was, a seventeen-year-old blonde with big tits and a lot of hutzpah.

One of the tables on the opening day was all white—uniforms, the U.S. Navy had finally arrived. Eight sailors who became regulars with daily visits, I called them "My Popeyes." It varied who came, but Popeye Mike was always there. He was 6' 2" tall, with green eyes, and dark skin from the sun after being at sea for many days. He loved history and was fascinated by Israel and what it had to offer for Christian people. He was very quiet, did not tell any dirty jokes, and only smiled when somebody else told one, but he never burst into laughter. I stood next to him once, listening to a joke being told, and everybody laughed and held their stomach, including me. Popeye Mike was the only one who only smiled a little. His eyes smiled just a bit, but not more than that. He drank like a champ, but he never appeared to be drunk. He always wore his uniform, which was white and spotless. He also smoked, Marlboro lights, which were very expensive at that time in Israel, and he always offered me a cigarette. He would wait for my break and smoked with me in the corner away from everybody.

I remember the first time he lit my fire—OMG...literarily, okay? —he used matches, and first of all, he got his cigarette going before he offered me a light. I asked him for the reason, as he was always such a gentleman, opening doors, helping me when serving the table, and doing anything he could to give me a hand.

He looked me in the eyes, and with his deep amazing voice and an accent that came from a small town in Michigan, he explained that the first person who lights a cigarette from a match also gets all the taste and bad stuff that comes with it. The second person gets only the fire. A real gentleman would never light a woman's cigarette first with a match. That was it. I was in love. Completely. He thought about me even when lighting a cigarette, and I loved his accent, which sounded better than anybody I had ever heard on TV, which was my only experience with English speakers until I met Popeye Mike.

I learned to like Budweiser. I had to try it with the guys at least once to understand what they were all so crazy about. I made sure not to drink while I worked after one night when it was so hard to read my hand writing that the bill came out a complete mess. No more beer for me during work became my new rule.

I was also asked not to take away the empty beer bottles as long as the guys who were drinking them hadn't paid their bill yet. They had an on-going competition. It was part of their outing—they were very thirsty and proud about it.

I made this mistake once, in the beginning, and cleared the table. It was the only time I saw these guys freak out. Well, almost.

It was also a good strategy on their side, and I got it. They could count bottles and compare who had what and could then control the bill. Smart. Although, I never saw them counting bottles and comparing with my bills. I was always paid with no questions and tipped very generously.

I came to work one day with a bandage on my finger. Everyone, of course, asked what happened, and I said, "I fucked my finger." This was a literal translation from Hebrew, and I thought it was a legit one in English as well. I found out it was not. I was so embarrassed when the whole table started to laugh. Everybody in the place looked in my direction, and I was the only one who was not laughing.

Popeye Mike was the first one to stop laughing. It was the first time I saw him really laughing. Now he was trying to get everyone else to stop as well, but they just wouldn't. The owner was looking in my direction and seemed very happy. What does he care? He sees a table full of empty bottles, with eight Navy guys laughing and having fun. So, what, if I'm standing there completely clueless and hoping that the earth would find a way to make me disappear?

Popeye Mike got up and took me to a corner.

"What did I say?" I asked him. I really wanted to know what everybody was laughing about. I knew I was funny but this?

"Never mind," he said, "they are just being stupid and drunk."

"No really." I repeated my request firmly. "What just happened? I can't go back to the table without knowing what I said, and besides, I want to say it again."

Popeye Mike blushed and tried to explain it to me in a nice way. "You see, in English, we use the, hmmm, this word that you used, not to describe the way you hang a picture, but something more between a man and a woman."

I suddenly got it! OMG, I was even more embarrassed, but it took me exactly two minutes to get over it and get back to work. "My tips are going to be sky rocket tonight," were my last thoughts. And I was right.

When I returned with more drinks and food, everyone at the table was very polite, and they looked at Popeye Mike while he thanked me for the drinks. I heard them laughing when I left the table. Popeye Mike was angry with them and told them to stop. *What a guy*, I thought as I smiled. When I looked at my bandaged finger, I smiled even more. I had learned a great lesson on how not to do a "straight translation" between languages.

The plane carrier was supposed to be in town for eight weeks, which turned out to be twelve weeks. Almost three whole months. During that time, I saw Popeye Mike almost every day—me as a waitress and him as my favorite customer. Not only because he always left a generous tip, but mostly because he stayed behind after everyone left, and the place was almost closed. It was just the two of us. He told me a little about his life and asked a lot about mine. Four years older than me, he was twenty-two and joined the service when he was eighteen. Exactly what I was going to experience. Popeye Mike did not have a girlfriend waiting for him at home, and I had just broken up with my boyfriend of more than three years. But we never did anything other than talk. I always had to run home, since the first of my three jobs started early. Popeye Mike told me he loved Israel and thought Israeli women were the most beautiful women in the world. I agreed with him with a warm smile.

On their last day in Haifa, all the guys who had ever come to the coffee bar since their first day in the Haifa port, gathered together at one table. They insisted on sitting in my section, and together, which meant a lot of noise and me running nonstop.

I served about twenty Popeyes that night, and everybody was very happy and cheerful. They had enough of Haifa and were happy to say goodbye and continue to their next port. Haifa is a great port and the weather was amazing, but they were missing the sailor's life, I guessed.

Popeye Mike was the only one who was quiet the whole evening, and he did not have his usual six Budweisers. He had only two and the traditional ice coffee the place offered. It was my favorite drink, and I used to prepare it for my special customers with my own special twist. Popeye Mike knew that, and often, when he arrived first, it was his first drink for the night, before all the others arrived and joined his table. If I had an extra left after I made his ice coffee—and I very quickly learned to get the right quantities to have a little bit left—I made it a custom to join him for a quick fifteen-minute break during my busy work in the place. Twenty minutes later, the place was usually packed, and I was running around for the next five hours, making sure my tables had the best service I could offer them. It was my pleasure and fun to do so.

That evening was completely different. Popeye Mike asked me to join him for a walk at the end of the evening, and I agreed. I waited anxiously for the end of the shift to arrive. I didn't care about the food, the drinks, or the tips so much that evening, and just wished I could leave everything behind me and escape the place with him while it was still busy. But I could not. I needed the money. It was my regular shift, and we were short-staffed, as all the restaurants were busy with not enough waitresses to fill all the shifts. It would all change the next day. It would be the last time Popeye Mike and I would see each other. We had never taken a picture together, and we had never held hands.

The place was completely crowded that evening, and time slowed while I ran around, thinking about Popeye Mike, catching him catching me looking at him and trying to concentrate on what I was supposed to do. At closing time, we needed to get everyone out. Surprisingly, the guys paid their bills quickly, kissed me on the cheek, hugged me, and said their goodbyes very fast. It had been a fun time, and we all had great memories. Popeye Mike was the last to pay and waited for me at the exit.

I decided to surprise him and asked him to join me in my car. We drove to the top of Carmel Mountain where I knew there was a view point and something even more exciting. There were benches with a view of the whole area—the port, the lights of all the cities around. It was a warm summer night with an amazing full moon. And it was private. Nobody was walking around in this area at almost midnight.

We found ourselves a bench and sat next to each other. The view was picturesque, and I was melting while sitting next to Popeye Mike. I had never sat so close to him before when we were alone, and he smelled so yummy. He suddenly turned and kissed me. I was so surprised that it took me a few seconds to understand what was going on. He was an amazing kisser, and it took a long time until we started talking again. He gave me a bottle of Opium, very fashionable and popular perfume for that time. It had a very high-end designed bottle. I knew it cost a small fortune, and I also hated the heavy oily smell.

I told him it was the most incredible gift that anybody had ever given to me. Let me pause here—I just learned what Opium perfume is made of. I was wearing a Curry/Thai/Italian dish on me.

Popeye Mike and I wrote to each other for the next couple of years. It was 1984, no internet, Facebook, or any other tools but mail, as phone calls were very expensive, and one could never know if the other person would be at home. In my case, my parents were the first to pick up the phone, and they didn't speak English. They knew about Popeye Mike, as many letters arrived, and they were not happy about it. I had a feeling that I wasn't getting all the mail that came from Popeye Mike.

I still had Popeye Mike's letters with me years later. It was exciting to get them, each time from a different place in the world. Popeye Mike even included a picture of himself in one of them. It was no joke. Pictures were a very expensive thing in those days and sending them to somebody meant something important. Now imagine from the middle of nowhere in the world, a sailor is choosing to send me, in Israel, letters and a picture.

Time passed. Seven years later, during which time I joined the army, did my service, got married to the same guy I broke up with before I met Popeye Mike, and divorced him two years later. Life is a bitch, and sometimes it has puppies. It was a peaceful friendly divorce, life was sweet and good, and it felt as if I had started all over again.

It was 1991, and the Gulf War had just started. I was a single young divorced woman, and often joined the parties on Tel-Aviv's roofs. We danced, drank, and watched the Patriot missiles flying in the sky. A dangerous place to be, as the Iraqis aimed at Tel-Aviv with their Scuds. Unfortunately, they did quite a good job, and Tel-Aviv was hit more than once.

My parents lived on the other side of the country, and they didn't know what I was doing. I had my own place to celebrate what might be the end of the world or at least the end of Israel. We were all very young—early twenties—and believed that nothing bad would ever happen to us. This was the feeling we had while dancing as the sirens went off, reminding us that we should be in a closed hermetic room with gas masks next to us in case of a chemical bomb. As I said, we were young, and nothing would ever happen to us.

Two weeks into the war, I received a phone call in the early hours of the evening. I had just returned from work. Not much was done those days, thanks to the war. Most people came to work and warmed their seat, as everybody listened and watched the news all the time. Whoever had a family outside of the Tel-Aviv area, already had left the area. The ones who stayed behind were a combination of those who did not have relatives to stay with or were young like us and did not care. Like me. It was the best time to go to the beach and to party. All the cool people stayed in town, and there was no traffic and no parking issues. Life was good.

I was waiting to hear about a party that night, so when I answered the phone and heard a man speaking English on the other side, I was caught by surprise. I recognized Popeye Mike's voice right away. The last time I had seen Popeye Mike was in 1984. The last time we were in touch was in 1987. It was four years later, and I had NO idea how he got my phone number. I had moved at least five times by then, and my telephone number had changed every time. No, there were no cell phones around.

International calls were crazy expensive at that time, and the lines were usually bad and often disconnected. I had an uncle in Pittsburgh who used to call once every couple of months, and those calls were always an adventure.

And now I was on the phone with a call from the other side of the world, and it was Popeye Mike on the line.

"Are you okay?" he asked.

"Of course, I am," I said. "Why shouldn't I be?" I was completely confused. I wasn't sure what was going on, and I still couldn't figure out how he had found me after all this time. What did he want from me?

Popeye Mike said that he was in the United States, and he was worried about my safety. He wanted to send me a ticket to come over, and because he was an American citizen, I could come at his invitation. This meant I could get my visa right away. He had already checked everything and made the arrangements, and all I needed to do was say yes.

"Everything is fine," I said. "I'm not going anywhere. I'm not leaving behind the country when a war is taking place. I'm not running away."

"Are you sure?" he asked. "Things might go really bad, and you can always go back."

"Thank you, but no thank you," I said. "I really appreciate it, but I'm not going anywhere." I didn't dare mention that a Scud had fallen three miles from my place the previous week, and a whole base of Patriots aiming from Israel to Iraq was located only a couple of miles north of my condo. Even my parents did not realize it.

Google Earth was not around at that time. I felt stormed. Popeye Mike had come back to my life and was asking me to leave everything behind and run away. This was not something I would ever do. But he was worried about me, so he was trying to get me safe and back to his life. What was going on?

"Okay, it is your decision, but we just want you to know that we are here if you change your mind. You can always come and be safe here with us."

Silence on the line. "Who is us?" I finally asked. The silence on the line was now longer.

"I'm engaged," Popeye Mike finally said. "We are getting married in three months."

Although we had not been in touch for four years, and I had been married and divorced during that time, I felt like I had just been punched in my stomach.

"She is standing next to me, and I told her all about you. She will be happy if you decide to come over here and be safe with us."

Again, with the "us," I thought.

"Mazal Tov, and all the best wishes in the world, Popeye Mike. I'm really thankful for your concern, but I'm just fine," I said, then hung up the phone. I did not have any way to get in touch with him. This was for the best, I thought. I felt bad, and I did not know why.

My life changed drastically in the next twenty-five years. I re-married, continued with more higher education, gave birth to two girls, and enjoyed an international career that had taken us as a family to different places in the world. We had lived in Montreal for eight years and moved to the Seattle area six years earlier. I had a prime office location with a view of the waterfront and a two-minute walk from Pike Place Market. To die for. I came to work every day with a smile on my face. I loved my job and the people I worked with, and I still used English phrases that caused people to laugh hysterically.

A couple of years ago, I received a request for a new connection on LinkedIn. When I looked at the picture, before I even saw the name, I jumped from my chair. It was Popeye Mike. He had found me. Again. We connected on Skype the next day. It was so easy to see each other and hear each other. Thank you, technology! He had gained thirty pounds since we had last met. He'd also suffered through a stroke. Popeye Mike had stopped drinking and smoking and was still married to the same gal who stood next to him when he called me twenty-two years before. My heart went crazy. I used to dream about this moment for years. I tried to find him once, with no success, years ago, and never tried again. Popeye Mike had one son, the same age as my oldest daughter. Popeye Mike had a very similar job to mine and lived in a house in the middle of nowhere in Arizona. His weekends were spent working around the house or BBQing with his wife's family. I told him what had happened to me during the past twenty-two years, and we tried not to think out loud about what could have been if we had ended up together.

We kept in touch; he reached out every time he saw me active on Skype—the Skype is the limit, was our slogan. We kept exchanging daily stories and family events. In the meantime, I broke up with my husband thirty-two years after I first met him, and I did not tell Popeye Mike a thing while we kept our discussions going. One day, he asked me how I was doing, and I knew I needed to share with him what was going on.

I told Popeye Mike that I was going through some difficult personal issues, and I didn't want to talk about it. Hurray to my decision to share with him what was going on. I asked to end the call, and he said, he "understood." It was the last time I talked to him. In the two years since that last call, I travelled to India, to Israel twice, bought a house, sold a house, moved to my own condo, watched my youngest graduate, and finalized my divorce.

I don't think I will talk to him again.

Sometimes the right thing is to leave things the way they were. Things have changed, and are changing, but we can't change the past. I started looking at an online dating account at the time we had our last call. I didn't want Popeye Mike to think I was flirting by telling him about the changes in my life. Thinking of him made me realize what I was looking for in my future partner. He made me feel good about men in general.

9 - I MOVED TO A GRAVEYARD

When I was in my late forties, I bought a condo. This purchase and move marked the first time I had lived alone in thirty years.

Do not misunderstand. I have sold and bought five places in my life, in Israel, Montreal, and Seattle.

And here I was doing it again, but my sixth place to own was a completely different experience.

I moved from the top of Cougar Mountain in Issaquah to almost the middle of the city in north Seattle. The commute changed from driving seven miles to the highway and another twenty miles to work to a seven-mile drive to work. I went from having an acre of lawn that I needed to trim and cut to a tiny patch of yard. I downsized from 2,500 square-feet inside space to a 1,000 square-foot condo.

I thought it would kill me to live in the city and to live in a small apartment. But, it turned out the completely opposite.

I loved the neighborhood I had lived in Mirrormont. All trees and woods, with the closest house half a mile away. I could walk naked on the deck, play loud music in the middle of the night, and nobody cared or heard me. Bears walked on my back property, and deer ate apples from the apple tree in the front yard.

When I bought the house with my husband, we had bought our dream house, the one where we would spend the rest of our lives, entertaining friends and imagining our daughters—seventeen and nineteen--with their own families visiting us. It was all so real and happening.

But plans change, and after the divorce, I lived in my own condo—I used to say condoms, until somebody finally corrected me—slept in my own bed that I shared with my dog and enjoyed a beautiful small garden that was my therapy.

The condo was located next to a graveyard—a mere five minutes' walk from Washelli Cemetery, a huge and very well-maintained cemetery. I hesitated in the beginning, even freaked out at the idea of going there, while on daily walks with my dog. One day, I decided to enter, and I fell in love. I loved the fact that it was so close to me and so green.

The cemetery was huge, and I saw it as a park to be used by the neighbors. I walked around and read the stones. There was a military area where all the stones looked the same. But one day, I saw a Star of David on one of them. I had found a family. It looked much friendlier right away. I felt I belonged. Jews everywhere, right?

The next time I walked in, I was with a date.

We just finished enjoying happy hour. We both lived in north Seattle and had dogs. It was a weird date, with a lot of silence, and I kept feeling that the guy, Mike #54, had something strange about him, but I could not point to what it was. But as I was attracted to the strange, I was intrigued.

Mike #54 was black, fifty-one, handsome and fit, loved beer, and smelled good. He did not look me in the eyes for one second. His eyes were always around me, through me, or on my body. I dressed up for our date. I liked to dress up a little for a date. In this area of Seattle, if you are not wearing jeans you are already dressed up. I wore a summer dress with small heels. My makeup was always in place, a gentle touch of an eyeliner, mascara, natural blush and a lipstick that did not go away for eight hours. Thank you, Cover Girl, I am a living proof for your commercials, even after eating and kissing. It did depend on how long the kissing lasted. I will have to get back to you on that.

We both had to take our dogs for a walk, so we decided to meet in the graveyard, and to continue the date we had just finished at an Indian restaurant during happy hour. The dog walk would be a kind of second date.

Eight o'clock during the summer in Seattle 2015, one of the warmest and driest summers in Seattle's history. The only place where the grass was green was the cemetery. Ridiculous. All these dead people must be very pleased. But for me, it was now an off-leash dog park, and that night also a second date location.

Mike #54 parked at the other side of the cemetery, so we met in the middle with the dogs. Mike #54 had a young Mastiff, only a year old. He was not fixed, very friendly, well built, and very horny. I believe that dogs have the same character as their owner. Daisy, my dog, on the other hand, was a five-year-old bitch, fixed, friendly like crazy and always going to the lips for a kiss. What breed was she? Only her mother knew.

We walked a little with the dogs on leashes and then decided to sit down and have a joint together. I always carried some weed on me, and Mike #54 suddenly woke up. After the first puff, he also talked, for a whole fifteen minutes without stopping, and he looked me straight in the eyes.

Mike #54 worked at the Boeing field, usually night shifts. The Boeing factory operated 24/7 and is one of the biggest employers in the country and in the Seattle area. It took me time to understand what Mike #54 was doing for his living during the shift. From previous experience, I have found when somebody is not clear about his job, it usually happens he isn't happy with the job or feels ashamed of the job, or thinks I have a better job—making more money—and is embarrassed. Happens a lot with men.

Mike #54 had a very physical job and had been doing it for a few years; hence, his unusual physical shape. Most men I met around his age drank a lot of beer and had a beer belly. Mike #54 had no fat on him. He looked very much in shape, and this was not thanks to a gym membership.

"What do you like best about your job?" I asked.

"I don't have to talk to anybody all shift long," was his answer. Wow, I thought, I have so bumped into the wrong person. But right then he was very talkative and smiled a lot. I always say weed is the solution to the world's problems! Or at least an excellent way to start a conversation. I am always a firm believer in natural drugs and besides, everybody takes something, so it might as well be something green, right? AMEN.

Mike #54 had a son who was nineteen and had just joined the army. It sounded as if we had a lot in common. My kids were about the same age, and one of them was in Israel, volunteering, and the other planned to go there the following year. I, myself, served in the IDF, as part of being an Israeli citizen. When I told Mike #54 I had been in the IDF, his face changed, and he looked at me with a very respectful expression. He liked the idea, and he was not the first man I had met who appreciated it.

In the meantime, we let the dogs run free when I realized we had a problem. Mike #54's dog, Diesel, was very aggressive and chased Daisy like crazy. Every time Diesel got to Daisy he tried to penetrate her, and Daisy would not allow him. I never saw Daisy running so fast and acting so afraid. I tried to call her to me, but she tried to get away from the young stud, and at one point, she went and sat under Mike #54's legs, shivering and scared. It was the only place that Diesel did not bother her.

I tried to get her out of her hiding place, but Diesel pushed me as well and tried to get to Daisy. Mike #54 just sat there and didn't do a thing. He watched but didn't respond. Was he so high? I questioned if that could be true. My pot wasn't that strong, so it didn't make sense that a big guy like him would be affected by a light joint. We shared the joint, right? But Mike #54 was not moving and not doing anything to help me and Daisy. Mike #54 sat and talked very slowly about his son, his dog, and his work that was "just okay," but he made enough money to pay the rent.

I could not take it anymore. Daisy shivered and shrieked under Mike #54's legs, Diesel was trying to get on top her from the behind. He jumped all over and hit powerfully—both Mike #54 and me— in every jump he took. But Mike #54 just sat there, mumbling quietly and still didn't move.

I stood and looked at Mike #54 still sitting. That's how big he was—we were now the same height—and I said that it was getting late, and I had a few more things I needed to do. At this point, Diesel jumped so hard on me that I fell on the ground. Daisy freaked out at that point and started to cry. Did you ever hear a dog cry? It was my first time, and it sounded awful.

Finally, Mike #54 grabbed his dog with both hands and put a leash on him. I was still on the ground and tried to get to Daisy, still crying for help, behind Mike #54's legs. I managed to put the leash on her and stand while taking few steps back. Mike #54's dog was acting crazy in his hands. He was a puppy and thought this was all game. I could not get Daisy to move. I stood up with the leash in my hands and tried to pull her away. She finally ran and stood behind me, while I kept on walking back. Mike #54 still sat on the bench, with Diesel going crazy in his arms. But Mike #54 was a strong guy, so he held Diesel tight.

I turned back and started walking very fast toward the exit of the cemetery. At one point, I started running, and felt my heart beating like crazy. I had to stop. Daisy was now jumping on me and trying to lick my face. I knew Daisy, this was her way to show her love and thanks. I let her kiss me as much as she wanted, because I had not done a good job. I hadn't defended her against Diesel. I promised her it would not happen again.

As a note to myself and to the future, I learned an excellent lesson. If the dogs do not get along, the owners will not get along as well.

10 - NO PLACE LIKE HOME

I met Mike #70 after an awful date experience with a black guy who accused me of being a snob and stuck-up after a few text messages and one date. When I Googled what "stuck-up" meant—I knew what a snob meant—I became distraught. I never, and at no time, considered myself as stuck-up. I considered myself entirely the other way around—someone who was generous and not judgemental and always very proud of it. How dare he call me that?

When Mike #70 and I arranged to meet, I decided that I was going to be as friendly as possible, not allowing the last date to impact my behavior to the wrong side, quite the contrary. A new person, a new day. I'm not stuck-up, and I don't think I'm better than anybody else.

We met online, on OKCupid, and I loved his smart-ass answers to the 1,936 questions that the site asked us to answer. He used long sentences, with words that I had to Google. He had a crazy sense of humor—a dry cynical

British style, the kind that I adored. He got me right away.

"You are a hip mom who needs to spend a night in the city," he told me. Exactly how I felt, so we met. Mike #70 chose the place, which was the Blue Moon Tavern. The Blue Moon was one of the first bars in Seattle, established in 1934, full of posters, books, and graffiti on the walls from famous dead people. The place was close to Washington University, and as such, had attracted a lot of colorful characters who became regulars and sipped a beer in this famous old establishment. Many famous dead authors used to sit there, and their books filled the shelves in the bar. Today, the Blue Moon is more of a dive bar, and the area is full of homeless people and students. But I'm not from here, remember that, so every piece of history and local story excited me and triggered my imagination.

I walked into the bar and was immediately impressed by the place. The men who sat at the bar looked so different from the men with whom I worked and who lived in my area.

I mostly worked with Indians from India or the local Seattle geeks, and the men from the area I resided in Issaquah were white, white, and white. Microsoft village lived in the suburbs, and I was part of it.

I fell in love with the Blue Moon the minute I walked in. Mike #70 left his bar stool and approached me. He opened his arms and raised them to hug me. A stranger in the middle of a bar. It took me a sec, but I hugged him back. It was a warm hug, and a great start to a discussion over a couple of beers and a shot of tequila. Mike #70 took care of the bill without saying a word. Just the way I liked it.

The conversation went great. Mike #70 had a very hot and deep voice, and he knew a lot about Seattle and the area. He enjoyed reading, cooking and was very interested in history and geography. He had lived in Germany for fifteen years and had traveled in Europe for his own pleasure during those years. *Wow*, I thought, *a worldly man*. Sounded very much like me.

Two hours passed quickly, and we both were starving. Mike #70 suggested that we walk to a Thai restaurant that he liked, which was near. While walking there, he told me about the places we were passing and the history of the area. Mike #70 had my full attention. He knew so much, and I always got hooked on guys who were smart. He also looked to be in very in good shape at 6' 1" with no extra fat on his body. He was skinny but masculine skinny. He walked fast, and I had to touch his elbow and ask him to slow down a little, which was a surprise for me, as I am known as a fast walker, and was always asked to slow down. Mike #70 looked at me, smiled, and apologized. Then he made sure he followed my pace. I never had to remind him again. The walk to the Thai restaurant took about fifteen minutes, and we passed many interesting sights. It was 6:30 p.m., the beginning of summer, and lots of homeless people were in the area, including teenagers, who asked for change every time we passed one of them. Mike #70 made sure I was safe, and if he noticed somebody who looked a little crazy, he switched his place with me, so he would be closer to that person. Mike #70 also explained to me what he was doing. I smiled and felt good about him protecting me. I liked to feel protected by a man. It was a new feeling that I never had experienced before. I made sure to tell him that. It was a very much appreciated masculine attribute in my eyes and in my heart. When I told him so, I could tell he loved my words. His eyes twinkled, and a little smile began to appear under his beard. Suddenly, he gave me a huge smile, and his beautiful green eyes looked so happy. I got this warm fuzzy feeling in my stomach, and I was enjoying the date very much.

While walking, a homeless person asked Mike #70 for a cigarette, while touching his arm. It was like they knew each other.

This was a very Seattle thing, the asking for small change or a smoke, but I never saw a homeless person physically touch another person while asking for something. Mike #70 gave him a cigarette, and said to the guy, "Good luck, man." Mike #70 then apologized to me and said that this guy looked like he really needed one, and usually he didn't give cigarettes away. I smiled. I liked generous, sensitive people, and again, another brownie point for Mike#70.

We arrived at the tiny Thai restaurant that held about five two-top tables and another eight seats in the bar area, which also served as the counter for the very small kitchen. The customers who sat at the bar could see how the food was being made right there.

We stood in a line outside with three other couples while we waited to be called into the restaurant. The staff greeted and smiled at Mike #70, and we were treated in an amicable way. Hmm, here we were in an Asian/Thai restaurant, but this was not the typical treatment from my experiences. Asian restaurant people are usually very stiff and correct. and the staff was usually very polite and showed no feelings when serving. Here it looked like they all knew Mike #70 and liked him. I asked Mike #70 why he was getting such respect and attention, and he explained that he loved their food and ate there almost every day. Wow, this guy was doing well if he could afford to eat out every day and have a beer before he went home. Oh well, I was starving, and the smell was just fantastic. Finally, we were asked to enter. We were seated at the bar, and Mike #70 explained what the cooks were doing and what kind of dish they were preparing. As I was married to a chef for many years, I found it interesting, but my ex never took the time to explain or show me anything. This stranger—who was apparently not a chef—knew so much and took the time to share this info. Another couple of brownie points.

We had a fantastic dinner, which Mike #70 chose for me. Hot but not too hot, steamy and lots of Thai flavors. Never had a dish like that before as it was a new cuisine for me, and I loved it. Tom Yum soup. Our discussion flowed, with no silent moments and with lots of laughs. Mike #70 ordered a Thai drink that was so sweet, I couldn't even smell it, let alone drink it. I'm not a fan of sweets. Mike #70 drank my drink as well as his.

Mike #70 had graduated from the University of Washington with a major in English and loved to read and cook. Since he had traveled all over Europe, we compared places we both had visited. Mike #70 had a very different experience as a local who lived in Germany for so many years, and his stories were fascinating, dangerous, and full of fun and crazy stuff. I loved his English. It was a cool-hip English sometimes, and a very academic one at other times. Depending on the subject, his vocabulary stretched and changed. I stopped asking him questions, as he always knew how to explain and give a background that was relevant to make sure I got it. Again, a brownie point for him.

Four hours after we first met, Mike #70 walked me back to my car. He made sure everything was fine and helped me settle safely in my car before we said goodnight. He checked the area quickly and looked around the car. His eyes were on me and on the street at the same time, the whole time. Our second hug for the evening was even better than the one that started our date, which was four hours earlier! His beard smelled funny. I never smelled anything like it. A combination of an old shaving cologne and something else, but I deleted this thought from my mind.

Before I left, Mike #70 asked me if he could see me again. I smiled and assured him that I would love to hear from him. But as I drove away, the unsettling smell followed me, became a part of me, and I wasn't sure what I felt about it. I am susceptible to smells and can throw up very quickly from a scent that does not go well with my nose or my stomach.

I felt I was about to puke and needed some deep breathing to get fresh air into my lungs. I was on the highway and had been driving for fifteen minutes with all the windows open, which meant an awful noise in the car, but the smell finally faded away. I rubbed some hand lotion on my hands and touched the area next to my nose. I felt better.

I arrived home with a smile on my face. It was a long drive, but the food had been delicious, and the company was excellent. The sixty-minute ride to the suburbs seemed like a treat and gave me some relaxation time. I kept thinking about Mike #70's deep voice, green eyes that smiled only when they looked at me, and the way he walked the streets like he was in a jungle. I never saw a man so aware of everything around him and all the time, like a wild animal that was looking for its way in the wilderness.

Later on, Mike #70 texted to ask if I had gotten home safely. I assured him I had and thanked him again for a lovely evening.

Mike #70 texted me again the next morning, asking if I could make it to the same place, at the same time that night. I was thrilled to hear from him, but I could not make it. I had another date scheduled already. When I told Mike #70 that I couldn't make it, I felt the disappointment on the other side of the line. I felt terrible and was saddened myself. I texted him to give me thirty minutes to see if I could change my plans.

I texted the other guy. I apologized and asked to reschedule, explaining that I had had a long day at work. He understood, and we rescheduled tentatively for two days later, promising to be in touch. I never heard from him again.

Later that day, when I arrived at the Blue Moon, Mike #70 waited for me, sitting on the same bar stool. This time, he kissed me on my cheek and gave me a long warm hug. I kissed him back, on the cheek, where he had no beard. The smell was there again, and it hit me hard. I could not ignore it.

We took a seat in the same nook where we had sat just twenty-four hours before, so it was now "our" seat. It was only the day before, but it felt like it had been ages ago, and we had known each other forever. We started talking. Stories, major life events, history, books, places around us, just talking and sitting next to each other. The beer and the tequila shot came very quickly, and we repeated the same routine by walking to the Thai restaurant with lots of smiles running between us. This time we held hands while walking down the street. I felt Mike #70's chest pumping and his posture rising. I enjoyed the fact that he felt like that next to me. I felt right about him and about us.

That evening, when Mike #70 escorted me back to my car, he held my head very close to his head and whispered in my ear, "You know, it is going to be something special between you and me. It is not going to be just a fling."

"I know," I whispered back, looking in his amazing green eyes. The beard had that smell again, and I couldn't figure out what the scent was, but I had smelled it before. I felt the vomit reflux coming back, and my stomach became upset. Was it the food? Something with his beard? I found it hard to put my finger on anything specific at that moment. I needed fresh air, which meant I had to get away from Mike #70. I quickly got in my car and drove away.

We kept seeing each other every second day. Mike #70 worked in construction, and Seattle was booming with it. New condos were being built everywhere in 2015. Mike #70 started his day at 5:30 in the morning on site, with one of the biggest companies participating in Seattle's boom. I did not like the architecture, ugly boxes, but Mike #70 was so excited about his job and the company that I did not say a word. He worked six days a week, from 5:30 to 4:30 or later, if needed. His schedule dictated our dates' schedule. Each date ended just before nine o'clock as Mike #70 needed his sleep.

We started having lunch together almost every day. I drove to his constructions sites, and we spent an hour eating lunch and chatting in the sun until he needed to go back to work, and I had to head back to my meetings. Seattle is a small city, and we were usually five minutes' drive from each other.

Every time we met for lunch, Mike #70 waited outside. He said that all the guys who worked on the construction site with him were very impressed with me and asked him a lot of questions.

"So, what do you tell them?" I asked him.

Mike #70 just smiled and said, "I tell everybody that I've met the most fantastic woman in the world."

I felt great and gave him a quick kiss on his cheek. That smell again.

On the days we had dates, it was after I had finished my daily job. I would drive directly to see Mike #70 at the Blue Moon. In those days, I arrived in downtown Seattle at nine in the morning and left Seattle around nine o'clock to get home at a decent hour to say "Hi" to the kids and go to sleep. I had a long commute to the boonies. Mike #70 always escorted me to my car and walked from there. He still refused my offers to drive him to his place, and said he loved to walk as it "cleared his mind."

Mike #70 didn't own a car, as he lived and worked in the city. This made complete sense to me. He also, always, carried his iPad with him in a large bag. He even had his own salt and pepper shakers that he liked. They were exclusive brands, which he took out in restaurants and used to flavor his food. Oh well, we all have our *shticks*.

He was knowledgeable about many subjects, a true intellectual, and we had lengthy discussions on diverse topics. We also became very close physically, and we enjoyed a lot of hot kissing and goofing around in the nook. Everybody knew us by then as a couple. When I walked in, the bartender knew my name and greeted me with a personal "Good evening." At this point, I also received an update whether Mike #70 had "clocked in" already or not.

One night, I asked Mike #70, again, if he wanted me to give him a ride to his place. He thanked me and said he enjoyed the walk. It was pouring rain when he said it. I insisted, but Mike #70 just smiled, closed the car door behind me, and walked away. I drove away, not sure what had happened and why, but there was nothing I could do.

Another date, another day, again, a passionate kiss and goofing around next to my car. We had been seeing each other for three weeks, and we had been in touch and saw each other almost every day. The smell changed after Mike #70 had a haircut and trimmed his beard. I learned a man with a beard could use either a special oil or an aftershave. We agreed to choose the scent together the next time he ran of what he was currently using.

One night, after we made out for two hours in the nook, I asked quite assertively, why he never invited me to his place. Mike #70 apologized and explained that he had awful roommates, and the apartment was always a mess. I smiled and loved his sensitivity.

We kept going out and eating in a variety of local ethnic restaurants, all within walking distance of the Blue Moon. The restaurants were not cheap, and a few alcohol servings were always part of dinner, which made the final bill high. Mike #70 was always starving and ordered a few dishes each time. He made sure to finish everything that was served. I used to sit back and watch him enjoying every bite. At one point, I told Mike #70 that I had decided not to drink anymore, as I was gaining weight, and I didn't like the feeling of driving home after a couple of beers almost every day. He agreed and loved the idea. The next time we went out, I drank water, and Mike #70 ordered "only one beer." He apologized when he ordered it, and said, "I need to unwind a little."

"You are a big boy," I told him. "It's your decision, and you can do whatever you want." Mike #70 had three beers that night, while I had only water.

A few nights later we met again at the Blue Moon. We both loved the place and made it a habit to start our dates there. It was Friday, and we started early that day at 4:30. I planned to stay in Seattle until 10:30. My girls were not home, so I was in no hurry. I would have loved to spend the night with Mike #70, and I knew that his work for the next day had been cancelled.

It was happy hour all over the city—one of the main reasons I fell in love with Seattle when I first visited during my business trips from Montreal.

We finished two beer pitchers, and each one of us had two shots of "our" drink, tequila—or, as my girlfriends call it: "To Kill Ya." We were entirely into each other and could not take our hands off each other.

But the smell came again. This time it came from Mike #70's beard, hair, hands, ears. I couldn't breathe. I pulled away from our passionate moment and asked Mike #70 to go out for a puff. Mike #70 smoked his long Marlboro lights, I smoked a light blend of weed and American Spirit tobacco. I never smoked anything else.

I knew Mike #70 worked in construction, and he hadn't had a chance to go home and take a shower before we had met. He apologized for his messy appearance. I just smiled and didn't say a word for few minutes, as I tried to stabilize my breath in the open air, between puffs.

"So," I said after few minutes of silence, "did you have a chance to see yourself in a mirror with a sink today? Your beard is combed, and I don't see any paint on your face or hands."

"Oh, I had a mirror." He laughed. "But I didn't have a sink, so I used the wet wipes, which we use to clean the floors to clean myself today. I made sure I was ready for my baby!"

Mike #70 said it proudly and reached out to me for a hug. I was sure I was about to puke at that moment. On him.

I turned around so he couldn't see my face. And while I tried to take a long clean breath of fresh air, I inhaled again the smoke I was trying to puff out from my homemade joints. I immediately choked. I lost my breath, and Mike #70 tried to reach out to me to pat my back gently and help me. He got closer, I took a step back and kept choking. At one point, I also started to laugh, which definitely did not help with the choking, and in fact, it just made things worse. Again, he took a step toward me, and I took a step back.

I finally relaxed and stopped coughing but felt sick. My face was red, and I felt like I was going to choke again if Mike #70 had gotten any closer to me. I pushed him away gently and asked him to give me few minutes to relax and breath.

"Please, just wait for me inside," I asked him with a smile, as much of one as I could manage, and he looked at me, smiled back and left.

After he went back inside, I took a long breath. My joint wasn't burning anymore, and I did not try to light it again. I needed to find a way to walk into the Blue Moon, sit next to him and...and what? How could I change his smell? Well, I always had a plan.

I carried with me "Renata's first aid kit." It had a small perfume, hand cream, small brush, mints, and a few other feminine things. Condoms were there as well, as a girl never knows what she might need, and I was prepared for anything that might come on my way.

I went back into the bar, and visited the ladies' bathroom right away, or what is called their "ladies' room." Mike #70 had told me that he once got "lucky" in the ladies' restroom with a woman he had met in the bar, and they broke the door while they were doing their thing. The door hadn't been fixed since then. I looked at that door and almost puked. The place was tiny, smelly, and looked like it hadn't been cleaned for ages.

Lucky for me, there was a clean, decent smelling piece of soap on the side of the sink. I made sure I washed up with the soap, including my face, hands, and everything else that had touched Mike #70. I wiped myself with some toilet paper and put on some hand cream. I sprayed the perfume on my scarf. If I had trouble breathing, I could put the scarf on my nose and mouth for first aid.

When I went back to our nook, Mike #70 was already ordering another pitcher. I told Mike #70 I had a great hand cream, but he needed to wash his hands first. Mike needed a lot of lotion on his hands, which were dry and rough from the construction work. I promised him a hand massage if he washed his hands.

Oh, the happiness on his face! Mike #70 rushed to the restroom, but not before he kissed my lips. It was quick, and I survived. When he came back, I noticed he had washed his face as well. *We have a good start here*, I thought. I helped Mike #70 wipe his hands and took out the hand cream. The third beer pitcher arrived, and we had our own isolated time. Mike #70 faced me, and I took one of his hands and started massaging hand cream into it.

While massaging his hands, I tried to broach the subject of visiting his place again. I knew that if we went there, he would have a chance to take a shower. This was the only thing I could think about at that point.

Mike #70 straightened suddenly, and brought both my hands together, looked me in the eyes. "I need to tell you something."

I hated these moments. These are never good moments. "I'm listening." I took my hands away from him and held them tight between my legs.

"I live in a half-way house," he said. What does that mean? I had never heard the term before.

"Mike #70, remember, I'm not from here, you will have to explain some more."

Mike #70 explained to me that he had not adjusted well when he came back from Germany, and he couldn't find a place to rent. He wasn't a druggy, although he used to be—cocaine—but he had been clean for the past twenty years and had not touched any drugs in that time. He finally found this place that would accept him, and this is where he lived— a half-way house. This was also the reason that he never wanted me to give him a ride or would not invite me to his place. Mike #70 said all of this in a very low, soft voice, and looked me in the eyes all that time, with his big green eyes. I could see that he was making much effort not to cry.

I needed to understand what was going on. Who was this guy I was holding hands with and had been enjoying for the past four weeks?

"So, you can't come and go as you wish?" I asked.

"No, I have to be there by 9:45 p.m., or they close the door, and I'm out. I have my own room, but it is minimal, and we all use one refrigerator, and everybody steals my food all the time, so this is why I eat out every day."

I was dizzy. The alcohol, the smells, and then this news.

"I need to go home," I said. I needed to think clearly. I got up to leave the place and kissed him on his forehead.

"You don't need to walk me to my car." Mike #70 had drunk much more than me, and he was not in a condition to walk. I promised him I would be in touch the next day, but I needed to leave, and it had to happen right then!

He looked confused, and his eyes filled with tears. I saw everything running through his eyes: pain, hurt, and fear. I hated leaving him like that, but I couldn't stay. Then I reconsidered. Maybe I should stay, just for few more minutes.

"I'm going to get a glass of water," I said. "Would you like some?" I dropped my bag on the seat. I looked at him. Mike #70 kept his head down, and he shook his head. I came back with one glass of water and drank half of it slowly. His head was still down, and he didn't say a word. He just looked down at the floor with his hands clasped together on his lap.

"Mike #70," I said, "look at me. Please look at me. What is going on with you? Do you really work every day in construction?" I thought that this was one thing I knew for sure, as I visited the construction sites for lunch so many times. Mike #70 was always coming out from the construction building while I was waiting outside. I wanted to start with something I knew to be true.

Mike #70 had even built a bench next to the entrance of one of the sites because of me. The bench was not part of the original plan, he told me, but his manager allowed him to put it there, as he saw me waiting in the car on a few sunny days, and there was no place to sit next to the building. What was really the truth, was suddenly the question.

Mike #70 didn't move, and I waited quietly. I looked around at the people who were drinking at six on a Friday night. The place was almost full. All the bar stools were taken, and people stood in a small line to get more drinks. There were no servers in the Blue Moon besides the bartender. All the regulars were there, and I had become a regular in the past month. OMG, I thought, I knew all the regulars, and the regulars knew me. One of them, an older guy with long white hair, always wore a leather jacket and a black leather cap, black glasses, and he looked like an intelligent man. He always sat at the bar and gave me a smile when I walked into the bar, making sure I saw him noticing me. He was always in the middle of a discussion with someone sitting next to him with a glass of beer in front of him. I never saw any of the regulars eat. The Blue Moon didn't have a food menu, and people were encouraged to bring their "takeout" into the bar and have a drink while eating it.

The dots started connecting for me as I sat there and thought about our dates. Mike #70 used to carry food from the Thai place and eat it here every day for the six months before he met me.

This was also where he washed his face and half of his body, quickly, before I met him after work. On this Friday, he had been late, and I was early, so he hadn't had a chance to do it. What was this guy going through, and why had I let him pay for all our outings?

"What else, Mike #70?" I asked him. "Please tell me everything. I need to know what is going on."

Mike #70 kept his head down with his hands clasped between his legs. I could not hear his voice. He spoke very quietly, and I had to get closer to him, so I could hear him.

"It's not a half-way house," he suddenly said. "I'm sleeping in a church that opens its gates to homeless people every night at 7:30. If I get there too late, I don't have a place to sleep, so I sleep outside. I need to be there by 9:45, or I'm out."

"What?" I stared at him. "You have no address? You are homeless?"

He raised his head, and his posture came back. "I am now, but I am getting out of it. I have saved four thousand dollars, and I'm looking for a place to rent. You will see, baby, I'm doing everything for you!"

I looked at him and had to think fast. I did not want to insult him, but what he just shared with me was just crazy, and I could not hold myself back. "You are doing *what* for me? No, no, no, no, this is not the case. You are not doing anything for me."

Now it was Mike #70's turn to be confused. "What do you mean, baby? I want you to be proud of me." He was dead serious. But so was I.

"Mike #70, who are you?" I asked him again. "Can you tell me the whole story and the whole truth? Did you really graduate from college? How come you know so much about so many things? And food, how come you know so much about food?"

Every time we had visited a restaurant or a bar, Mike #70 had been very knowledgeable about the food, the origin, the ingredients, and as an ex-wife of a chef, I appreciated his knowledge and found it fascinating that he was so into it. It was something that we both shared — a love of ethnic foods and the history behind them.

Mike #70 started to talk, still with clasped hands now on the table, reaching for his beer every couple of minutes, and his eyes fixed on some dot on the wall on the other side of the room.

He moved to Germany when he was in his early twenties. He became addicted to cocaine while in college, and it continued afterwards. Mike #70 managed to stop his addiction, by himself, twenty years before, and he had never done drugs again. At the time we dated, he was forty-six years old.

He met his only wife, a German lady, at a party in one of Seattle's clubs, and she was a few years older than him. She was a tourist visiting from Berlin and was looking to have fun. She decided to stay with him in Seattle and moved in with him a couple of days after they met. She was a cocaine addict as well.

Six months after she moved with him, her mother came to see what was going on with her daughter and tried to convince her to go back to Germany with her. The girl refused to leave Mike #70 behind. The mother offered to pay for Mike #70's ticket if he wanted to go back with both of them to Berlin. Mike #70 agreed. He had nothing to lose. Mike #70 had been raised by a single mother, who was eating herself to death. His mother had not left her house for two years and was getting bigger and bigger. At one point, when she had to go to a hospital, the paramedics had to call for help to get her out of her bedroom window, as they could not get her out of the door. The fire department took care of it.

Mike #70 moved to Berlin with the girl and her mother. They got married then divorced a few years later with no kids involved. Mike #70 decided to stay in Germany, as he did not have enough money for a plane ticket, and there was no reason to return to Seattle.

Mike #70 worked in a variety of jobs as a taxi driver, UPS driver, pizza deliveryman, you name it all the while earning low wages. Once he'd been stabbed by a Turkish man. He told me it was a hate crime, and it almost cost him his life. He showed me a big ugly scar on his chest, a souvenir from that incident. Mike #70 spent three months in a hospital recovering, and it took a couple more months, out of the hospital, to get back on his feet and return to work.

Mike #70 lost all his money and all the property he had, as his place was broken into and everything was stolen while he was in the hospital. Mike #70's landlord hadn't heard what had happened to him, so he got rid of Mike #70's furniture and anything else he found in the place. When Mike #70 came back to his home, it wasn't his place anymore. It was rented to somebody else, and Mike #70 had to start from scratch, with nothing.

As an immigrant, and thanks to the fact that he was once married to a German citizen, Mike #70 applied for Germany's generous social security program. Mike #70 then found a job as a UPS driver and started driving all over Europe with his new position. He said that this was the best time in his life, as he had a car, rather a delivery car, and some of the trips took a week or more. To save money, Mike #70 would sleep in the car and use public restrooms to maintain himself. He said this was when he grew his beard, as shaving every day became a hassle, and growing a beard made more sense for his lifestyle.

Then, three years ago, a high school sweetheart had found him on Facebook. She had just lost her husband a few months before and reached out to Mike #70, relying on their love story when they were eighteen. She paid for his plane ticket back to Seattle, and he moved in with her. Mike #70 came back to his homeland with nothing, after fifteen years in Germany. His mother died after his return, and he sold all her belongings and bought a heavy silver ring. This was all that was left of her, a thick silver ring on his right hand. I had noticed this ring before, and I finally understood its special meaning and value for him.

The relationship hadn't worked out, and Mike #70 found himself in the streets, with no job and nowhere to go to. He had lived on the streets ever since, which was about two years. He had found his current job four months ago, and since then he had been sleeping in the church every night. He had managed to save money, and he was on the waiting list for a half-way house.

"Why don't you just rent a place, with a roommate?" I asked very naively. In my world, you could move and do whatever you wanted when you wanted.

"I can't," he almost shouted at me, looking around to see if anyone had heard him. "I have no address. Everybody asks for an address, credit history, and a credit card. You can't have a credit card if you don't have an address."

Good point, I thought. I had never known anyone who didn't have an address. *The man without an address*, I thought. It almost sounded like a horror movie title. But this was no movie. It was my reality, and it was about the man I had been so into for the past four weeks. So many thoughts ran through my head, and I could not control any of them.

Mike #70 talked more about his mother; he repeated himself, and I did not stop him. It was a way to confirm everything he had just told me, and I listened to his words. His mother had died few months after Mike #70 came back to Seattle. In her last days, she lived in assisted housing, and Mike #70 had taken all the money that she had in her purse and bought the ring. He held up his hand to show it to me. It was a strong massive silver ring, and he wore it on his right hand. That was all that was left from his mother, the woman who had given birth to him and raised him. No pictures were left, nothing from his childhood was saved to remind him where he came from or the woman who had raised him. His father had disappeared when he was a year old, and he never had any connection with him.

"But it is all changing now, baby." Mike #70 grabbed my hands and held them next to his chest. "You are with me, and everything will change." Mike #70 looked straight into my eyes and held my hands on his chest, and I could feel his heart pounding. I didn't know what to say. I took a sip of his beer and handed him the glass so he would leave my hands alone. The beer grabbed his attention for a couple of minutes while he sipped, and my hands were free. I wanted him to stop holding my hands and looking into my eyes. I just couldn't be touched by him at that moment.

We drank the rest of the pitcher and were very quiet for the next hour. I then kissed him goodbye, said that I was tired and promised I would meet him the next day for dinner, as we had previously planned.

This time, the way home was very long. It was a Friday night, and traffic was light. The highway was almost empty, and I felt as if I was in a different world. Everybody was already home, sitting with their families for dinner. I knew that both my girls were babysitting, which meant they had left the house an hour earlier, and the house would be empty and quiet. I needed this quiet time. I had to understand what was going on with me, what was I doing with Mike #70, and how I had managed not to have any red flags and bells ringing all this time. Was it the alcohol we consumed when we were together? Was it the exciting conversations? I decided it was a combination of both, as I'm a complete sucker for a smart guy and a shot of tequila. The perfect combination to get me horny, and I was all yours.

I was never stuck-up, but this was really a lot to digest. Who the hell was this guy I was exchanging fluids with for so long? How safe was that? Me and a homeless guy? Yes, he did have a job, but he had been homeless for years and lived on the streets. I proved to myself that I was not stuck-up, and I'm very human, but this was really too much. Did I have too much compassion in places where I should have red lights in front of me? This was not like me.

I got home and hugged my beast. Daisy is always happy to see me, and I felt a little better for few minutes when Daisy tried to lick my face and made me hug her and give her a belly rub. This was Daisy. My Bitch.

Whoever will be around, I will always be her master, and I didn't ask for it. Daisy was the world's gift to me and my daughters. She reminded us every day that we are not alone, and we were loved with no conditions.

I took a long shower and just crawled slowly into bed. I was in a safe place, but my mind started to run crazy with thoughts, now that I was alone. Pictures from the dates we had together, a few sentences Mike #70 had said, and I didn't understand at the time, were all coming together and making sense. I remembered his comments about his last girlfriend who was crazy, and he said he had saved her from the streets. They had just broken up a month before we met after seven months of being together. He said she was crazy sick. What did she have? He did not say, but I vowed to ask him.

I decided to let it go for the moment. I wanted to understand what crazy means for Mike #70, and I had a bad feeling about what his answer would be. I was also afraid to hear the rest of his story, but on the other hand, I was dying to hear more, and learn more about this guy. Mike #70 had managed to get himself up and back to normal life, more than once, and he had fooled me for so long that I wanted and needed to know more about him.

I had so many questions, but I couldn't concentrate because my thoughts were all over the place. My stomach hurt, and I didn't know if I wanted to puke, or if I should get over it while breathing slowly and taking deep breaths.

I tried to meditate. It did not help, so I decided to try and puke.

It was the first time that evening that I just let everything go. I puked my guts out, and I started crying. I had a Déjà vu of the scents that I always smelled when out with Mike #70.

I suddenly remembered the moment he told me how he cleaned himself that afternoon before coming and seeing me. I cried harder. I puked and cried. I hated myself for feeling like that, but I couldn't control it. I got a puking urge every time his image came to my mind. I was on the floor, next to the toilet, my head leaning on it, while I kept crying and puking for a long time. I could not get myself up on my feet. All the beer we had drunk was now coming out of me, and it smelled and felt awful. It reminded me of Mike #70's smell, and I vomited more and more. At one point, there was nothing coming out of my stomach, and I felt the acid take over my throat. Every move was painful. Every thought was painful.

Mike #70 and I did not meet that weekend as planned. I asked him for some alone time, and it was the first time I was happy he didn't have a car. It would have been hard to stop him from coming over to see me. Mike #70 was very disappointed but didn't say a word. He was not in touch the whole weekend, and finally he sent a message on Sunday evening, asking me how I was. I wasn't doing very well, but I did not say a word and instead asked him if he wanted to meet the next day on Monday. I had a plan, and I wanted to share it with him. I thought it was a great plan, and I was sure he would be very happy to hear and cooperate.

At that time, I worked in downtown Seattle next to Pike Market, in a very modern office building on the waterfront. We had locker rooms at work, including showers and all the amenities one needs after going to the gym. I thought that Mike #70 would be able to take a shower after his work day and use the clean, free towels that were offered there. After Mike #70 cleaned himself, no excuses this time, we would go up to my office and have dinner that I would prepare in advance and bring from home. We had a beautiful open space with a scenic view of the waterfront. The best view in the city, as I always said. I thought it would be a suitable place to sit and talk: quietly with no pressure and no alcohol.

Mike #70 was thrilled and agreed immediately. That was it, I thought this was the solution. When we went out, Mike #70 could come to the office, take a shower, and then we could start our time together. This would eliminate any odor issues.

Monday arrived, and I was excited to see Mike #70 but not in a fun way. We had a lot to talk about, and we needed to do it immediately. But shower first. It was after working hours, and I was sure nobody would care or would be there. I got the men's locker code in advance and sent Mike #70 in, while I waited in the lobby, sipped my coffee, and played with my phone.

Suddenly, I saw a man burst out from the men's locker room. He ran to the other side of the corridor. I knew the guy; he worked on the same floor as I did. Two minutes later, he came back with one of the building's maintenance workers, and they both marched very fiercely into the men's locker room. Something had happened to Mike #70 while he was taking a shower, and now he needed help, or maybe a bad discussion had taken place between these two men? Or maybe Mike #70 had done something stupid like trying to mess with this guy's things? I had a million theories running in my head, and each one of them was worse than the other. I decided to continue sitting there and not move from my place while I waited for Mike #70 to come out, as we agreed.

A few minutes later, the maintenance man and the guy who worked on my floor, came out from the lockers, murmuring among themselves and looking at me. Or at least I felt they were looking at me. I had worked in this building for five years, and everybody knew me. While they stood there, Mike #70 came out behind them and walked directly to me. Mike #70 had a little limp that made a cracking noise when he walked. You could hear his limp in the silence of the building's lobby, as it was after business hours and there was nobody else around.

I got up and asked Mike #70 if all was fine. He nodded, and we walked toward the elevators to go up to my office. The guys still stood there, now apparently looking at us and talking between them. I prayed, deep in my heart, that this incident would not create an issue for me in the office, but I couldn't do anything about it at that point.

I worked for an international company that used a lot of security, and the building was very secure. The elevators would not run if you didn't have an employee badge. Once we got on the elevators, Mike #70 would not be able to go anywhere without me and my employee card. I explained it to Mike #70 while the elevator went up.

"Mike, what happened in there?" I tried to ask it quietly, although I was nervous like crazy.

"They knew I was homeless," Mike #70 snapped back at me. He had never snapped at me before.

"How did they know you were homeless?" I tried to understand.

"They just knew, okay? I don't know how. The guy with the beard was looking very strange at me when I walked in, and suddenly he left and came with a guard."

"Did they say anything to you"? I kept asking.

"No, but they were standing next to the door waiting for me to leave, so I did everything very quickly and left."

"I'm sorry," I said to him. "It must be a tough feeling to live like that." Mike #70 did not answer.

Suddenly, he grabbed me in his arms and said very softly, "But it will all change with you."

We got to my office floor. I had an office on the fifth floor with a fantastic view just next to me toward the whole waterfront. You could see west Seattle from our building on a good day, and from the other side, you could see Mount Rainier. I was usually very thrilled and excited to show these views to visitors, but this time I just wanted to end the night. I felt weird, and I did not enjoy our time together. We still had to go through dinner.

I had brought some cold cuts, bread and butter, and hummus that I had made from scratch and lots of veggies. This was the first time that I had fed Mike #70 and not the other way around. I saw Mike #70 reaching for the food like he hadn't eaten for days. He might not have eaten for a couple of days except for beer and nuts, like he used to do. Mike #70 apologized for his hunger and said that everything was so good that he couldn't stop himself. I just smiled and let him continue to dig into the food.

Mike #70 stopped when he tasted the hummus. He said he had never tasted such a tasty hummus and made me tell him the recipe. I knew that Mike #70 was into cooking, so I felt very proud and dictated the recipe:

2 cups cooked chickpeas (aka garbanzo, aka hummus! This is the Arabic name for these beans)
¼ water or bean liquid
1/3 cup tahini
1/3 cup olive oil
½ lemon – you can always add more later
½ tsp cumin
2 garlic gloves
¼ tsp salt, but be careful. Adjust to taste

Combine all ingredients together in a food processor until smooth. Allow to chill in the fridge for couple of hours, to get the best flavor. Pita bread and Israeli veggies salad is the best thing to serve with the hummus.

Mike #70's first question was if I had ever tried to add cilantro to the mix. I told Mike #70 that my hummus is a religious issue for me, and nothing should be changed. Let my hummus go.

I hardly touched anything and watched out the windows, as the night settled over the city. We chatted about everything and nothing. I could not make myself ask him any hard questions, as he was looking at me so hopefully and appreciatively. He was clean, smelled great, and his stories about Seattle's history, while looking at the view, took my attention to different places. We ended the evening by me dropping him close to the church where he spent the night. I drove home with lots of deep feelings and could not stop thinking about how he must feel when he walked the streets homeless. Everybody knew he was a homeless person.

A couple of weeks later, my kids were planning to sleep over at their father's place. It was the first time that I had had the house to myself since we had broken up six months earlier. Their father finally had found a place to stay and could host his kids. I decided to take this opportunity and invited Mike#70 to spend the night at my house. I knew he would love it. A real bed, real life, no need to wake up early and leave, as the church had stiff restrictions in place. At seven in the morning, everybody was out, and it didn't matter if it was the weekend or not. People had to leave until seven at night when the doors opened again.

Mike #70 had to take a bus from downtown Seattle to the park and ride to the east side—about an hour plus ride. I would pick him from there. When Mike #70 arrived, he looked tired and dirty. It was the first time I had seen him that dirty.

"I'm sorry, honey," he said. "I took the bus right after work and didn't have a chance to wash myself. This is the first thing I would like to do if you don't mind when we get to your place."

I didn't mind. In fact, I did not mind at all. Mike #70 smelled awful, and I could not get my breath going right with him sitting next to me. I had to wide open all the windows. Lucky us, it was early summer, and the weather was nice and warm.

I explained to Mike #70, very carefully and slowly, in the seven miles we had from I-90 to the Mirrormont neighborhood, that this house was going to be sold, and all the money was going to the mortgage. I knew what people felt and thought when they saw my house. We drove through Issaquah downtown, a beautiful area. Mike #70 smiled while looking at me, and he put his hand on my knees. I usually enjoyed his touch, but at that moment I was in an almost vomit stage, and I hated myself for that. And him. I smiled back and said that I couldn't concentrate like this. Mike #70 smiled back and took his hand away. I felt as if a ton of weights had been lifted from me.

Mike #70's eyes kept looking and running around while we drove up the mountain and got deeper into the wooded area. He didn't say a word when I parked. I had an electric car, which is really cheaper than other cars, but people do not realize it. The house, the car, the neighborhood, it all sends signals of wealth. Very false picture.

Mike #70 tried to kiss me when we walked in, and I gently pushed him away and ran upstairs. He came running after me. I took him to the bathroom and asked him for his clothes. I thought I should burn them. Maybe later. Mike #70 smiled his gentle smile and got undressed. He had a muscular body, and it was the first time I had seen him naked. A beautiful tattoo of Ganesh—the elephant-headed God—covered his back. He had no fat on him, exactly what I had imagined all this time, and all the other body parts were amazingly brawny as well. If he just would take a bath. I asked Mike #70 to start the bath and promised him a fresh towel. Thirty minutes later, I still heard Mike #70 in the shower. In the meantime, downstairs, I prepared us dinner, and ran a load in the laundry with only Mike #70's clothes. The clothes stank like crazy. Construction guy, hard worker. Added to the fact that Mike #70 had only two sets of clothes, and he didn't take a shower every day. There were so many things I took for granted, and I should not.

When Mike #70 finally came downstairs, he looked amazing. He always wore jeans and a cool T-shirt, and now he smelled fresh and clean.

Everything went amazing. Mike #70 drank like a fish, but we were not driving anywhere so who cared. In bed, he surprised me and was gentle and firm, while he kissed all my body. Oh shit. It was so worth waiting. We fell asleep completely exhausted and smiling. We woke up when the birds started their day. Well, I woke up and made sure that Mike #70 woke up with me. We repeated last night's activities and fell asleep again. It was the weekend, and we were in no hurry.

Mike #70 decided that he would prepare breakfast. He opened the fridge and started taking things out. I was surprised. I was married to a chef for twenty-plus years and never imagined that another guy could really do the same. Eggs Florentine, garlic butter on toast, chopped veggie salad and cottage cheese. That's it. I was in love. My ex hated cottage cheese, and I had to brush my teeth after eating it if I wanted to kiss him. Freedom! From "cottage free," to "free cottage!"

We spent the day together, walked around the area, played with my dog, and the day was about to end. My kids would be home soon. I drove Mike #70 back to the bus station. Mike #70 did everything he could to stay, but I could not let it happen.

When we got to the Park and Ride, we found out that we had missed Mike #70's bus by two minutes. It was the last bus for the day.

"I guess you have to drive me back to downtown," Mike #70 said.

I could swear that he was smiling under his beard, and this whole delay had been planned. There was no fucking way I would drive to Seattle, so I decided to chase the bus.

Ten miles later, we caught the bus when it stopped to take passengers on at Mercer Island bus stop, just off the highway. I blocked the bus, and Mike #70 ran out and got on it. Later on, Mike #70 texted to tell me the bus driver had been upset and very angry that I had blocked him and told Mike #70 hat I had committed an illegal act. Oh well, this was not the worst thing I've done in my life.

We still met on a daily basis, and slowly more stories came out. He smoked cigarettes only, no weed or anything else, as the company he worked for ran random drug tests.

Mike #70 made sure to stay clean, and his dream was to get accepted into the construction workers union. This was his only dream at the moment. He made a *very* nice salary and was always generous when we went out. I knew he could afford it, but I still felt weird about it. Mike #70 wouldn't let me pay for anything. We agreed that at least when we shopped for food in a grocery store and cooked together, I would buy.

When Mike #70's birthday arrived, we had been dating for two months. He wanted to visit the University of Washington's bookstore as a birthday date. Although it was Mike #70's birthday, he bought me two books. As I said, he was very generous and was doing everything he could to show me that he cared.

We went back to our discussions and talked about a place for him to stay.

When I asked why he had lied to me about where he resided, Mike #70 admitted that he was ashamed of his situation in life and did not want to lose me. Mike #70 said he never had a woman like me before. He was not the first man to say it, and I felt that with him it would be different.

A few weeks later, my girls planned a road trip to Vancouver, Canada. This meant they would be leaving the house very early on Saturday. They would be away from Saturday to Sunday late at night.

The girls went to sleep early on Friday, excited about their coming road trip spending the weekend in Canada with friends and driving alone for the first time.

This was our opportunity to spend another night together. Well, maybe even two without the girls around. I had a plan.

Friday nine p.m., I picked up Mike #70 from the Park and Ride bus station near my place. We went to the local brewery and enjoyed a couple of hours of good beer and greasy food. Mike #70 knew all about the local beers, and he had some lengthy discussions with the server. I was proud. The man I was with knew so many things. I had no idea what they were talking about, but the server kept coming with samples and offered Mike #70 more and more beers to try. Mike #70 drank everything that was brought to the table. Most of the beers were IPA, and I hated IPA. I'm a blond beer person, and I let him indulge in every sip. Anyway, I was the designated driver.

We arrived at my house after midnight. I had a plan in place and was very excited about it. I shared it with Mike #70 while we were having drinks, and he thought it was a great plan.

I had a small shack, like a mother-in-law unit, which used to be a workshop, built by the previous owners. The place was a stand-alone just next to the big house. There was no heat or water, only electricity. At that time the shack was full of things I had removed from the house and wanted to donate or throw away.

On Thursday, a day before Mike #70's arrival and my kids' trip, I cleaned the place and made Mike #70 a bed to sleep on the floor. I created a "bed" from a mountain of blankets. The plan was that we would arrive late at night from our outing, and Mike #70 would sleep in the shack, and I would wake him up and take him to my bedroom as soon as my kids left the house.

We got to the shack and went under the blankets. We could not stop making out, as we would have frozen if we had. It was cold, dark, and I was amused by the whole situation. I went back to my bedroom at four-thirty, and the minute I heard my girls leaving the house, I ran back to Mike #70 and brought him inside. It was 5:15 am when my girls left the house. Mike #70 took a shower and fell asleep the minute his head touched the pillow. We had a very relaxing weekend and said goodbye on Sunday evening.

Besides Mike #70 in my life, it was also the time I was getting ready to sell my house. It was a big house and needed some touchups before going on the market. Mike #70 was a construction guy, which meant he was the right man at the right time. My luck again. Mike #70 came over one weekend while the girls were home. I introduced him as a friend who had come to help. The young one left to her activities, and the older one stayed. She told me he was strange. I said that I knew he was different, but he was a good man, and I liked him for that. Mike #70 fixed few things around the house and had dinner with us. I saw that my daughter was not happy with his company, but Mike #70 was my guest, and she had nothing to say about it. She left the dinner table very quickly, and I drove Mike #70 back to the bus station, this time checking the schedule myself and making sure we were there at least ten minutes in advance.

At one point, Mike #70 started to text me every half an hour, and I asked him to stop. I had a job that I needed to do, and he was supposed to be busy in his position. I did not want to see him so often anymore, and I was tired of sneaking around and trying to guess if he would take a shower before our date or not. His stories were not so exciting, and his knowledge and familiarity of the city had lost their spark. Now I knew why he was so knowledgeable—he had the time to walk around and sit in the library and read when he hadn't had a job or a place of his own to stay. The library and the bookstores, these were his second home, after the bars that he visited every day.

I decided to take a weekend for myself. I had a Groupon that I had purchased a few months before for a cabin in a nowhere place—Tenino—fifteen miles from Olympia at Offut Lake resort, with the "Lady of the Lake" fishing area on site. I told Mike #70 that I was going away by myself. He did not believe me and kept asking me who I was going with. I promised him that I was travelling unaccompanied, as I needed to get away from everything and have some time to think.

It was Friday at noon when I started my road trip. I had a four hours' drive to get to the cabin, which according to the pictures I saw, was surrounded by trees and a lake. Very romantic place. While registering, the girl who took my details was very surprised I had come by myself, and that I was not into fishing. Oh well, this was my weekend, so no, it was only me there, thank you. I'll take the keys now. The cabin was tiny. Even for one petite person like me. I had no business staying inside for too long though. I found myself wandering around, writing, reading, and coloring a picture book I had brought with me. The cell connection and the Wi-Fi were sporadic, which meant that in some parts of the area it worked, and in most of the area, it didn't. Every time I got to an area it worked, I saw a text message from Mike #70 asking me how I was doing and what I was doing. I texted Mike #70 back, thanking him for his concern and assured him I was doing just fine. A couple of hours later, I looked at my phone again, and there were four text messages from Mike #70. The last text message said that one of his coworkers was from Olympia, and he could get a ride with him. He would be on his way to me in couple of hours. He asked me to pick him in Olympia. Fifteen miles from where I was.

I was shocked, upset, and pissed off. At no time had I invited him to join me. In fact, it was the other way around. I was very clear I needed this time for myself. I did not text Mike #70 back.

An hour later, the phone rang, and it was Mike. He was agitated that I had not texted him back. I explained to him that the connection was sporadic, and the fact that the phone just rang was a miracle by itself. Not such a good miracle, I thought.

Mike #70 told me he wouldn't be coming, as his co-worker had decided to stay in Seattle and not drive back home to Olympia. I felt such a relief, as if the universe read my wants and thoughts, and organized everything to make sure I could continue with my "monk time." It was the first time in my life that I had taken the time to be alone, and I was enjoying it. Mike #70's earlier message that he was on his way had shaken me a little, but I was back to my peaceful mindset with his news.

"I'm sorry to hear it, Mike," I told him. "I'm back tomorrow, Saturday, early in the evening, so maybe we can meet for a drink before you have return to church for the night."

Mike #70 snapped back. "Come and pick me tomorrow from Seattle and take me to your place."

"I'm sorry? What are you saying exactly?"

"I want you to come and pick me up when you are back, and I want to spend the night with you at your house," he continued, drawing out the whole plan, and how it should work.

"Mike, you know my kids are at home. We discussed it many times already."

We had talked about it more than once. When my kids are at home, no man would stay for a sleepover. Until now, Mike #70 had understood my decision, and I thought respected it.

"I don't care!" Mike #70 snapped. "Tell your kids that I'm your boyfriend, and I'm coming for the weekend. If they don't like the idea, it's their problem, you are their mother, and you decide for them. I'm important to you, so show me."

The birds stopped chirping around me, and the sun suddenly had this large cloud covering it. I felt like somebody had hit me with a brick and my vision went blurry.

"Mike #70," I said, trying to stay calm, "you are important, but these are my kids, and it wouldn't be the right thing to do. They are teenagers, and this is an agreement between them and me. They know their mother is dating men, and they date as well. We all agreed that nobody would come to sleep at our home."

"You are just bullshitting me." Mike #70 was yelling now. "I'm your man, and they have to accept it!" The yelling continued on his side, but I was not listening anymore.

"Goodbye Mike," I said and ended the call. The birds suddenly started chirping again, and the clouds moved from the sun. I turned off my phone and shoved it deep into my bag.

On second thought, I took my phone out, turned it on, and blocked Mike #70's number.

11 - MIKE MOTEK

I usually give nicknames to people, pets, and things that I really liked. It made me happy to use a nickname. It made me feel closer to them as if a pleasant memory had surfaced.

Mike Motek was one of those people to whom I'd given a nickname. He was also a perfect example of how pictures, texts, and talking on the phone cannot be replaced by a face-to-face meeting.

Motek is used in Hebrew, the way honey is used in English. It means sweet.

I always hated when guys "honeyed" me, many times without even meeting me. Just as an endorsement. In Hebrew, I had the same reaction, as the word is used mainly in the streets, when a stranger, usually a man, is trying to flirt with you. Do not *Motek* me, I used to say. I am not *Motek* at all!

I met Mike Motek on Plenty of Fish online dating site. He had an awful picture of his back, which was full of tattoos. I usually hated tattoos. Another image of him was taken in Hawaii eating an enormous hamburger, again a terrible photograph. He had long salt and pepper hair pulled back in a bun and a beard. And I hated beards since my time with Mike #70 and his awful beard smell.

His texts were concise, and usually contained LOL in every line. I knew I was funny, but really? There was nothing else he could say? So, Motek started texting HAHAHAHA instead. Obviously, he was not my type. I loved men who texted a whole paragraph and could face the same in reply. I always believed that this said a lot about the person on the other side.

And then came the weekend. We had already been texting for a few days, and a "get together" made sense. I wasn't very excited to meet Mike Motek, but I was bored and had no plans for the weekend. I accepted Mike Motek's invite for a Friday dinner at a new local seafood restaurant, not far away from my place, which meant a thirty-minute drive for me since I was still living in the boonies. Close always meant thirty minutes while I still had the house.

I was recovering after a toe operation—my third one, which deserves a horror story by itself—and still limped while wearing a medical foot sandal for a month. Not the sexiest performance in the world, but other than that, I had nothing better to do, and I did not have any expectations. This was going to be dinner, and that was all.

I parked too far away. On a regular day, I would not care, but at that point, I was in pain. I realized my mistake only after I left the car and started limping up the hill. I was already late, and my limping walk would make me even later.

I finally finished climbing the hill that had seemed like a small mountain. It was seven o'clock and dark. At least it was chilly, so I wasn't sweating too much despite my hot flashes! I saw the restaurant just across the street, and I was very relieved. I could not wait for my first glass of wine and to elevate my leg.

When I crossed the street, I noticed a handsome man smoking outside the restaurant, not far away from the main door. He was not much taller than me. I liked tall men, but something in the way he stood and smoked made him very sexy and manly. He had a ponytail, not very long, and from far away, and with the darkness going down, I saw the way his jeans fit him very nicely, and his shirt looked stylish and complimented his figure. He looked very much like the Marlboro man.

I walked to the restaurant door and took a second look at the guy. He had beautiful blue eyes and a beard. He smiled at me, and I smiled in return and turned back to open the restaurant's door. I suddenly heard my name from the back. I turned around, and it was him. My date was the guy with the ponytail, big blue eyes, and who looked yummy in his jeans and elegant shirt. He had been waiting for me while smoking a cigarette outside.

I lost my breath for a second—and no, not because of the cigarette as I enjoy a puff as well—and turned around with a huge smile. "Mike?" I asked.

"Yes, hun." He smiled back at me and stared into my eyes. Then I really lost my breath for a second. This had never happened to me before.

I lighted my own smoke, and we moved a little bit further away from the door, so we wouldn't disrupt the traffic of people going in and out of the place. When Mike Motek spoke, I could hear the sound of waves. He had this deep bass voice, accompanied by many years of smoking. He used words and phrases that I had never heard before, like "hun," "right on," "busier than a two pecker Billy goat." I loved it. I had never heard these phrases and asked questions about the goat. Mike Motek explained it to me, which made me laugh.

Mike Motek had already arranged for a table for us, and we were taken to our seats once inside. I ordered a glass of white wine; Mike Motek ordered ginger ale. Wow, I didn't expect a guy that looks like him to order ginger ale. When we received our drinks, I asked Mike Motek if he was going to have a toast with me. Mike Motek gave me a beautiful smile, took his ginger ale, and toasted with it. He tapped his glass with mine, and I thought I heard him say "Le'Hayim."

"Hun," he said to me after we had tapped our glasses, "I don't drink any alcohol, for twenty years now."

"Any special reason?" I asked, direct as always. I didn't like to BS.

"Yes," he said. "The alcohol made me do stupid things, and I behaved in wrong ways."

Wow, a man who knew his boundaries and was working with that to be better.

"So, you don't have a problem that I drink next to you?" I asked very gently, willing to give up my glass of wine, even though I had craved one so much during the past hour.

"Not at all. You drink whatever you want to, hun, don't you worry about me."

We ordered our main course, and Mike Motek tried to convince me to have an appetizer. One glance at the prices, and I declined politely. Mike Motek caught the look I gave the menu and announced very clearly, "Cutie pie, you order what you desire and don't worry about a thing." I smiled; it felt funny. His voice and eyes were all over me, and I was grateful. Still, I hated to order expensive dishes when it was a first date for three reasons.

1. You never know who was going to pay.
2. You never know if your date who wants to pay, really has the money to pay for it.
3. You never want to look greedy. This is not how I wanted to present myself.

I refused, politely with a huge smile, continued gazing into his eyes, and ordered only a main course. We continued the discussion while waiting for our orders to arrive. Mike Motek was a former submarine officer and had spent twenty years with the Navy. He had been honorably discharged, five years earlier, and since then, he had worked as a civilian for the Navy. Mike Motek was a contractor, and usually had projects of six months' length and more when he relocated to different areas in the States and worked in the local shipyard.

I also learned that Mike Motek had driven more than two hours to meet me and would have to drive the same distance back to his place. And yes, he really wanted to meet me. I was very flattered and blushed a little. I ordered another glass of wine.

Our food arrived, and while we ate, I saw Mike Motek's face suddenly covered with pain.

"What's wrong?" I asked. I stopped the discussion and put down my utensils. Mike Motek didn't answer me for a couple of minutes, while holding his stomach, and then suddenly he sat up straight, smiled at me and assured me nothing was wrong.

"This is not nothing," I said. "Something is wrong with you. You are in pain."

"Oh, it comes and goes, and I don't have time to take care of it." I gave him my Polish/Israeli mother pet talk, but hey… we had just met, and he was still smiling at me and letting his blue eyes roam over my body.

We finished our dinner and decided we wanted to spend some more time together. We were in my hood, so I was in charge of our next stop. I left my car behind, and we continued to my favorite wine bar in Issaquah, Vino Bella. Everybody knew me there, and that evening I was walking in with the handsomest man in the room. I knew everybody was looking at us, and I LOVED IT.

Mike Motek ordered a latte, and I moved to coffee as well. It's not fun to have wine alone. And anyway, I liked the idea of less alcohol. Not needed. We ordered one dessert to share. It was a private moment between us — sharing from the same plate. Mike Motek sitting next to me, smiling and then taking me to the dance floor.

A small eighties' band played that night, and we arrived when they were about to finish their show, which meant some slow dancing. Mike Motek smelled of fresh shampoo and soap, which surprised me, because by this point he had smoked at least four times already. His hair was smooth and had a nice feeling when my cheek touched it. He was 5' 7", which meant to me at 5' 2" that we were the perfect fit for dancing. Hmm... what a great surprise. I never would have imagined it from our online meeting and texts.

We went back to our coffee, and I saw Mike Motek once again hold his stomach while his face cracked with pain. I let him go through it, and when he touched my hand, I gave him shit.

"Well, how can a grown person be so irresponsible? You are about to drive two and a half hours home. What is going to happen to you in the middle of the night and the middle of nowhere, when you get the next pain attack?"

Mike Motek smiled, held my hand, and asked me not to worry. He said the coffee must have affected his stomach.

"Oh really," I said, "you don't know me. I'm Polish/Israeli and a mother; worrying is my existence!"

We said goodbye after telling each other, how much we had enjoyed the evening.

Mike Motek asked me if I was available the next day and wanted to know if I would like to meet again. I loved him for asking that. He was so straight and honest.

"I would be thrilled to see you again," I said, and we promised to be in touch the next day to schedule when and where. A quick butterfly kiss on the lips and off I went. We had just spent three hours together, and it was great.

The next day, Saturday, Mike Motek was the first thing I had on my mind when I woke up. What a fantastic date it had been, and what a surprise as well. I had gone on the date with no expectations, and it had turned out to be just great. I could not wait to see him that night as well.

At around eleven, I started to feel anxious. No sign from him. Around noon, I wondered if Mike Motek had woken up that morning and hadn't had the same thoughts as me. Where was he?

At two o'clock, I got the following text message: "Hi, Hun. I'm in the emergency room. It ain't the coffee."

Mike Motek had gotten home the night before but drove himself to the hospital in the morning. He had had another pain attack, which took place while he was talking to his mother on the phone. When his mom heard him in pain, she asked him what was he so busy with that he couldn't go to the hospital. His only plan for the day had been to see me. The smart woman made him, finally, go and get some help.

Mike Motek was diagnosed with stones in his liver and was about to go into surgery in the next couple of hours. He would be admitted for the night. If everything worked fine, he would be released the next day on Sunday.

I told Mike Motek I would be there the next day and refused to listen to any of his "you don't have to, hun" messages.

"Mike Motek, I'm a mother of two kids who are traveling, and I'm a world traveler myself. I know how it feels to be all by yourself far away from home and not feeling well. I don't have to be there, but I want to be there, and you don't owe me anything. Don't worry about it. It is just a human gesture that I feel I want to do."

I still had a lot of pain from my toe surgery, but I drove on Sunday more than two hours to the hospital. I took with me a small poster with a cartoon of chicken soup with matzah balls, thinking about the smile on Mike Motek's face when he saw it. Jewish Mother or not?

When I entered Mike Motek's room, he was sitting on the bed with his back to the door. He was texting on his phone, wearing a hospital gown. PINK. It was a PINK hospital gown! Of course, I could see his whole backside with only two small ties on the top, but all the rest was open. His hair was down and looked amazingly soft. I walked into the room and cleared my throat. Mike Motek turned around, saw me, and his face brightened. He started to get up on his feet, so I rushed over and tried to stop him. There was a nurse in the room, a lovely Philippine lady.

"Good morning," she said. "You must be the girlfriend. He was talking about you all the time."

Oh, really? I looked at Mike Motek while putting both my arms on his shoulders, trying to push him down on the bed. Mike Motek refused my efforts, stood up, and gave me a big hug, a long one, and whispered in my ear, "I'm so happy to see you."

It took us a couple of hours to get him released and be on our way home. Well, to Mike's place. But first, we stood in the parking lot to have a smoke. There was no question about that.

Mike Motek's car was parked in the parking lot, so I followed him, about thirty-minutes away. We decided to stop on the way and buy some food, as Mike Motek's fridge was empty. I showed Mike Motek the chicken soup cartoon. He loved it. He laughed like crazy and had to stop to cough in the middle. Heavy smoker. This made us decide to buy some chicken breasts and make a schnitzel. It was to die for. The idea of cooking together, I mean.

That was the day that I told Mike Motek that I thought I would call him Motek. I explained to him what Motek meant in Hebrew—honey, sweetie, but it really depends on how you say it. With the right tone, it does not sound so sweet—and he loved it.

The next few weeks, I received a "good morning" text message every day. Motek made sure to use Hebrew in his texts, like *Boker Tov Motek* (Good morning, honey), but I kept telling him that Motek was his name, not mine.

He refused to listen. We compromised: Hun was me, and Motek was him.

Motek was an alpha male. He did not have to do anything, wear anything special, or swear. He just was. Motek had a sexy cat-like walk, and his voice always made me feel like a woman. There is something in a deep manly voice with a cigarette's hoarseness.

Mike Motek had been a hard worker all his life, and a very early riser. He started his workday at six in the morning six days a week. In the one and only time I had spent the night at his place, I heard knocking on his door at 5:40 a.m. I decided to ignore the knocking, as it wasn't for me. Motek, on the other hand, decided to grab me even harder under the blanket and squish me a little. It felt good enough to squish him back. I could hear the knocking on the door increase in intensity. Motek completely ignored it and was all about massaging my behind. I had no problem with this. I could play deaf if I needed to.

At one point the knocking on the door turned to banging. Loud ones. Mike Motek stopped his moves, raised himself away from me a little, and then roared like a lion, "Fuck, I'm coming." I was not sure what he meant until I saw him jumping out of bed. He and his carpool were late for work. Everybody at the shipyard heard the story and had something to talk about for the next couple of days.

Although Motek didn't drink, he spent a lot of his free time in bars, around the shipyards where he worked. He was tattooed all over his back, with some more on his legs and arms. Each tattoo was a different story and life event. Did I already mention I don't like tattoos? Well, I loved his.

When we walked into a bar, I could feel and see people looking at us. The guys usually took a step back and gave us space. Motek was very protective about my injury and always made sure I was comfortable and feeling well.

We were in touch on a daily base. Mike Motek even took his first sick day in his life just to have lunch with me. This was easy. He only needed to drive thirty minutes to the nearest ferry, take a ride for forty minutes to Seattle's waterfront, and there I was. My office was just five-minute walk from the boat. Then, on his way back, Motek stood on the ferry's upper deck, jumped up and down and waved to me. Yes, he was the best alpha man ever.

In our daily texting, I learned that Mike Motek really hated the whole world. He was very hurt in his personal life and did not have a very optimistic view of the world. I was, on the other hand, Miss Give Me Lemonade and Some Vodka, Please, could not get it. With me, he was this teddy bear, and at work, he was the guy who everybody hated and fought with. Every day, he shared a story about another fight that had taken place that day. He had high work standards and would not compromise on anything. "My way or the high way," was his motto.

Two months into our dating, we talked about being exclusive and agreed what we had was great for both of us. Mike Motek kept warning me that he would hurt me in the end, and I kept asking him to shut up and enjoy the ride. A text message in the middle of the day was part of our routine to check on each other.

A couple of days after our talk about exclusivity, I got the "noon hello." This time, the text message was different. "Shalom, hun. I got kicked off the project. I'm leaving in four hours because I have a flight to catch."

Yes. That was it. Motek left four hours later.

12 - DOUBLE DIPPING

I had just broken up with a guy I had dated for four months, but during the last two weeks of the relationship, we saw each other only once, although we lived very close to each other. I had not wanted to break up with him in those two weeks because he was looking for a job and was very insecure and dependent on my comments and support. He didn't have anybody else to turn to. I thought I should be there for him and decided to be a "good person," and wait until he got on the horse again, which meant until he got a job. Then I planned to break up with him. Our relationship had become boring, and I started to feel he was taking advantage of me.

But what I didn't realize was he was lying to me all the time. He was not on the verge of saying, "Here, I got the job!!!"

He had received a rejection from a potential job a week earlier, but instead of telling me that, he kept saying that he was busy and had another interview and another interview with the same company. It all made complete sense in the world of five phone interviews before you actually met a person face to face or via Skype. Don't ask me how I found out, but I did and was very upset and disappointed. I was very hurt at first, but then I started to get mad. In the two weeks that Mike #75 had lied to me, I had felt sorry for him and was stressed. This, in Yiddish—one of my native languages—made him a *schmok* and me a sucker!

Two weeks of Mike #75's ongoing stories about how busy he was with constant interviews, while at the same time calling and texting all day long, made sure I was waiting for him.

And all the while, I made sure that he knew I understood and supported him.

But then came the truth, and it slapped me in my face. Zbang! Mike #75 was a liar. It was the second time "zbang" in this relationship.

It wasn't the first time I had caught Mike #75 lying, but the first time it made sense. When we met, online, Mike #75's profile he said he was fifty-four-years old. Mike #75 looked handsome, was in shape and just came back from twenty years in Central America, where he had a great career in the nature film industry. He was an artist in his soul, played percussions with a local Latin band, and was a great dancer. Everything about him sounded great and looked inviting.

A couple of months into our exclusive dating, Mike #75 told me he was turning sixty the following month. He only told me about his real age because a huge family party was planned for him, and he wanted me to join him. I asked him to explain to me why he faked his age. Mike #75's answer made a lot of sense. He felt young and was, physically, in great shape. He used to be a body builder when he was younger, and it still showed. Mike #75 knew that no forty-something woman would want to date an almost a sixty-year-old man. His sister-in-law finally opened an online dating account for him and put in his account information. Once you open an account, you can't change the year of birth info. That is the rule on the site.

It all came back to me when I found out the truth about what was going on with his job interviews during the last weeks of our relationship.

I decided that I had had enough. I was respectful and supported Mike emotionally and financially. I had paid for all our outings in the previous month. This was a lousy deja vu from my marriage scene.

When I finally broke up with Mike #75, over the phone, his reaction made me roll my eyes.

"But we'll still stay friends, right?"

Even at this point, Mike #75 didn't have the guts to tell me that he hadn't gotten the job. I mumbled something and ended the call.

The breakup call took place a day after I had my first "crowd surfing" experience. The only downfall was that the crowd wasn't there. I fell from a stage and cracked my head the day before I finally made the call to end things.

At that point, I was part of an Improv school and took classes how to do Improv. This was already my second semester, and I had been having the time of my life. Each week was hilarious and funny, and I thought that I had found something I loved to do and would be a part of my future—well, as a hobby at least.

The lessons took place in the Unexpected Productions' Market Theater, which is in a beautiful old building in Pike Place Market. The Gum Wall is right next to the theater's entrance. If you've ever been to this site, you know how disgusting it is, but it was also an attraction for laughter. God knows what makes such a place appeal to so many people who come there to stick chewing gum on the wall, stand next to it, and take a picture. I've seen brides and grooms, in their wedding outfits, taking pictures next to this wall as if it was a charming picturesque view. Oh well, different people, different tastes, different chewing gums.

I fell off the stage at the fourth class of the semester, and the group members already knew each other on some level. We started to meet earlier on the days we had a class for a bite and drink before we went to the theater. It was a cute—and very much younger than me—group of people, very local and white. I was the only one who had an accent, and the only one older than thirty-two. I also had the craziest sense of humor and laughed at myself the whole time. Pure fun.

We finished our happy hour for that day and went to the theater. As we were in our second semester, we were allowed to use the main stage, and it felt amazing to be on it—almost like performing in a live show.

Each class started with some warmup exercises to get our mindset in place and to bring everybody on board, repeating techniques that we were taught during the previous class.

We stood in a circle and had to say a short sentence, starting with the last word that the person before us had used at the end of the sentence. It was a rapid game, and you had to be entirely invested in it, as you couldn't miss a word. My turn was coming quickly, and I had to listen very carefully and take it from there. The sentence had to make sense, which was the only requirement—no gibberish allowed.

Of course, in games like that, the sentences that were thrown into the air were hilarious, not always logical, and we all laughed and enjoyed it. The person next to me had just started a sentence with a frog, and the last word was flying. When you say your phrase, you have to enter the circle, and when you end your sentence, you have to step back to your place in the ring.

I remember my sentence went something like this, "Flying happens when you are as high as a kite," and then I stepped back to my place, while everybody laughed. I was very proud of myself and acted fast to step back to my position in the circle to keep the game going.

I took one step too many and too fast. I was suddenly flying in the air from the stage to the floor, hitting my head on a piano next to the stage. I hit the floor, landing on my back and staring at the ceiling.

The next thing I remember was the quiet. Nobody moved. Suddenly, everybody was around me, and one of the guys ordered me not to move. Something ran down the back of my head. It had a wet feeling. I touched it and looked at my hand, which was red. Blood. No panic.

I sensed many things happening around me, but I was on my back and could not see anything. I slowly tried to get myself to a sitting position. I took a minute to assess how I was doing. I really wanted to close my eyes, but somebody was shouting, "Stay down and open your eyes," and anyway, it was too hard to do anything at that moment.

There was too much noise around me, and I needed to get out of there. I once more tried to bring myself to a sitting position, but two strong hands pushed me down, ordering me again not to move.

"Stop," I said to them, "just let me get out of here so you can continue your class." I hated to be the center of attention in situations like that, and I found it more helpful if I could just get myself to a quiet place.

I got up slowly, leaning on a steady hand that supported me. I started looking for my purse, while the teacher asked me to come with him to the room behind the stage. There was a couch there, and I could lie down and relax.

"I need my purse, give me a second," I told him, and one of the girls promised me that they would get it to me right away, and I shouldn't worry about it right then. I followed the teacher behind the stage and refused to use any help that was offered to me. "I'm okay, don't worry about me, just continue with the lesson," I kept telling everybody.

When we got to the promised sofa, I collapsed. I felt dizzy, and I saw black spots dancing in front of my eyes. I could not open my eyes, and I started to vomit. This was when the manager of the place decided to call an ambulance.

I don't know when exactly the 911 call was made, but for me, it felt as the paramedics were there in no time. The problem was that we were in an alley, and an ambulance could not drive to the door. The theater was located on a narrow and small alley—memories from old Seattle.

The paramedics walked in with a stretcher. I could not lie down on it because the theater walkways were too narrow as well. I needed to go down the stairs and walk all the way out to the main street, Pike and First, before I could lie down on the stretcher. I climbed the stairs back up and then back down to the alley, where an audience had gathered when the ambulance arrived. Everyone waited to see what had caused all the drama.

I asked the paramedics to continue walking to the ambulance and promised I would get inside and lie down once we got to it. The idea of the paramedics, dragging me on a stretcher, for fifty feet when everybody was looking was more painful than just walking by myself.

On the way to the hospital, the paramedic repeatedly asked me "proof of identity" questions and made sure I didn't fall asleep, while I repeated my declaration of being so tired and wanting to sleep. I was asked for my medical insurance, which I handed over very gracefully, from my purse that had been brought to me. I could not afford another drama by losing my wallet.

When we got to the hospital, the ER staff was already waiting for me, and had all my medical information with them, as the paramedic provided them with my details from my medical card while we were driving there. Wow, professional process and sweet action in place. The business analyst/nerd side in me was always coming out. I had a good feeling that I was in good hands. I would be out of there in no time.

I was told that I had fractured my head, and I would need a few stitches. About six. I had to wait for one of the doctors to come and see me. This part took some time, as they were all busy with more severe patients at that moment.

"Do you know anybody you can call who will come and be with you?" the nurse asked. I thought about Mike #75 right away. He was officially my boyfriend at that time. I decided that he was the last person in the world I wanted to ask for help. So, I called my kids, who I knew were with their father for dinner. This meant that my ex-husband would know what had happened to me, and HE was really the last person in the world that I wanted to see. My biggest worry was to make sure that HE did not feel or think that HE was needed and supposed to arrive with the girls.

I called my oldest, and surprisingly, she answered. She usually didn't answer phone calls. It was my lucky day. I briefly explained what had happened and where I was and asked her if she could come over and be with me. She promised that she was on her way. "Wait," I told her, "please do not tell your father where I am and what happened. I don't want him to come. Promise me that." She promised me, and I put the phone away. I finally could close my eyes.

I'm not sure how long it took my daughters to arrive, but they were suddenly next to my bed. I explained to them where I parked the car and gave them the keys. My youngest just got her drivers' license so she could take care of my vehicle. Another problem solved. I could close my eyes again. My youngest left to drive back home.

The noise in the ER was loud and did not stop for a sec. Although my eyes were closed, and there was a curtain around my bed, I heard and felt the drama behind the curtain. The nurse walked in again, greeted my daughter, and explained that a burn case from Alaska had just arrived, and all the medical staff was occupied with this situation. I didn't care; I just wanted to close my eyes and sleep. The nurse asked me how I was doing. She had to repeat it twice, as I was not answering. I opened my eyes and smiled briefly, "I will survive," I said, "just let me sleep." She did not like my answer and saw that my pillow was full of blood. The nurse left the room in a hurry, and suddenly I heard her again next to me. This time somebody accompanied her. She had come back with a doctor. I listened to her giving a brief description of what had happened to me, but I could not even open my eyes to see who was standing there and what the doctor looked like. Maybe he was single, I remember thinking. I will find my hero here in ER, where my head is bleeding. Nice first date story. Great story, I finally decided. Something to tell the grandkids.

"Miss Lubinsky," came a deep manly voice, "can you hear me? Can you open your eyes?"

With a vocal sound like that, how could I keep my eyes closed? I opened my eyes, and in front of me stood a young doctor who looked like he was in his late twenties. OMG, they are making them younger and younger these days. I smiled.

I tried to get to a sitting position, but the doctor pushed me back gently and asked me to relax and roll over onto my stomach. I followed his request. I did it very slowly and carefully, as I felt that my body was going in one direction, but my head was not following the same trend. I finally made it, so the back of my head was exposed to him. The doctor cleaned my head with some stinky stuff, which burned. I released a small sigh. My daughter held my hand all this time. I was so lucky I had her beside me; it would have been awful to be there alone.

The doctor finished the exam and said six stitches were needed.

"Can I go home after this?" I asked him, and he assured me that I would be able to go home, but my head would hurt a little, and then I would need to relax at home for two weeks.

I let myself fall asleep until he came back and started working on my head. Before he started doing it, he asked me if I wanted any painkillers.

"No, thank you, doctor," I said. "The only pain killer I take is marijuana."

He laughed and said that I could do that later when I left the hospital.

My daughter scolded me in Hebrew. "Mom, you are crazy, you just told him you are smoking weed." This was before weed was legal in Washington.

"So what? I didn't say I need a drink, a thing that I'm sure he would have overruled right away. I just told him I want to use some weed later on, as a green painkiller, and he agreed that this might help, instead of using processed chemicals." My daughter sighed.

The stitches were not so bad, and fifteen minutes later, it was all done. "Mazal Tov," the doctor said. "You have six stitches, and in two weeks, you need to visit your doctor to take them out. Please make sure not to fly from any stages from now on." Both of us grinned. My daughter did not think it was funny and told him that she has a crazy mom. I assured him she was right.

We finally got home, and I went straight to bed. I was not allowed to wash my hair for the next seven days to make sure the stitches stayed in place and the wound didn't open. Later that night, I woke up and thought I had had a nightmare. I had to touch my head to feel the bumps and to realize that this was not a dream. It had happened for real.

The next day I posted on my Facebook page a short description of what had happened to me, and that I would be in bed for the next few days. Although Mike #75 was my friend on Facebook, I heard nothing from him. Zero. I was surprised, and at the same time also offended and angry. I just spent the past two weeks trying to be kind to this guy and support him in his life, and he didn't even have the integrity to reach out and see how I was doing? Oh well, it was always good to know who the person was behind the mask. True colors, they say?

So, I made the breakup call, and I was very relieved. Then I changed my status on Facebook. My status had been in a hidden mode for some time now, so the change did not trigger any drama, as the only person who got the message about it was ex-Mike #75.

Facebook was a great tool I used to stay in touch with many friends and family around the world. But if I used it wrong, it could become a real pain in the ass. I was always cautious when using Facebook or any other application where I shared information and opinions. I followed the theory of imagining the person sitting in front of me. Would I still say the same? Great rule.

Two days after my injury, I became very bored. Crazy bored. I was not used to being in bed, and there was nothing I wanted to do. I did not like watching TV, I could not concentrate on reading, and I found myself on the online dating site. I disabled the account while I was dating Mike #75, and it had not been in use for the past four months. I reactivated the account and started surfing the profiles there. I also added some beautiful profile pictures from the previous week's road trip to a countryside. Surfing the site was my way of "people watching," as I could not leave the house.

One of the profiles got my attention. It belonged to a handsome man, fifty-six-years old, according to his profile. He mentioned that he was tired of all the profile patterns out there, and he would be happy to find a woman that knew the difference between their, there, and they're. I laughed. As an immigrant with English as my third language, I made sure I was not making these kinds of mistakes in my daily life and especially at work. In everyday life, I had an accent, so whatever I said sounded different, and I could hide behind it and laugh at myself. But at work, I had to provide the most professional level I could and compete with locals, while writing documents and communicating in emails. I knew damn well the difference between the three.

I decided to write him back, not as a candidate but just as a joke. I wrote, "I know the difference between the three, but I have an accent, which might not be okay with you."

Mike wrote me back right away, and we started texting each other rapidly. He had excellent English, of course, and I apologized in advance, for any grammar or spelling mistakes I might make, explaining to him that English was my third language. I also explained I was in bed after a head incident, so anything I said could not and should not be held against me. Mike responded with a laughing emoji in his text message and assured me that

I was doing just fine. He also took the time to ask about my condition, and he asked if anybody was with me and taking care of me because if not, he would be happy to come over with some food and provide me company. I assured him that my kids were taking good care of me, and we continued texting, and finally decided to meet a few days later for breakfast, when I would be feeling better. I already felt better with the thought of meeting him in few days. The plan was to meet at a local diner not far from my place.

This was Mike Security. Or in short, Mike S.

Mike S worked for the federal government, in a very high position. His career, on a daily basis, was to make sure that everybody in the United States was safe. Part of his job included screening people. He had a deep voice and a sweet laugh. Mike S was 6' 6" tall. We joked about my height and how we would look together even before our first date. I was thinking about how it would work in bed, and I could not stop smiling to myself while imagining it. Mike S promised me that he loved petite women, and I promised him I would buy a ladder.

In the meantime, I was approached by another suitor who got my attention right away. He was sixty-years old, very handsome, and wrote funny and yet very assertive messages to me. He was fascinated by that I had served in the Israeli army, as he had been a general in the Marines for the past thirty-five years. I never dated a Marine or a general before, and I got excited. We planned to meet the next day, which was Thursday. I will call him

Mike Marines, or for short, Mike M. I was double-dipping dating.

Mike M lived in a condo in one of Seattle's suburbs, next to a river, and he asked me to pick him up from nearby, where he was helping a friend put a fence in place. Mike M was about to be discharged from the Marines. His new career would be teaching science at a local college in his neighborhood.

I usually didn't like the idea of picking up a new date in my car, but Mike M sounded very military and trustworthy, so I decided not to follow my rules. He explained he had just retired from the Marines and in the process of settling down and becoming a civilian. Buying a car was a part of the process. I understood, and it made sense. I was bored like crazy from lying in bed with the stitches in the back of my head. I still had six business days until I could go back to work and sit for nine hours a day doing my job. I intended to at least take advantage of this time and enjoy it. I could not read for very long periods of time, and the TV was giving me a headache. The only thing I used for my pain and my mind were my regular joints, but I needed some company as well.

Our date, Mike M's and mine, was planned at a fun Italian restaurant not far from where I would pick him up. Mike M assured me that he would be clean and shining for our date. He worked outside—physically—the whole day, and he wanted me to know he would be considerate of my feelings. Since Mike M had been a soldier for most of his life, he knew how to get himself ready. OMG, he sounded so serious, a little too serious.

Mike M finished with "Sweetie, I really want to meet you. I have a good feeling about you." I usually did not fall for this crap, but from his mouth, it sounded genuine and sweet. I was under the influence of a head injury, so I was obviously not thinking clearly.

When I arrived to pick up Mike M, he was already waiting outside the house where he was working and waved at me with his hands very enthusiastically. He wore a sleeveless shirt, appeared to be in great shape, and in general, just looked very good for his age—much better even from the pictures on his profile.

He got into the car and started chatting right away. He was glad I was there, he was delighted to see me, and he was pleased to say that I looked terrific. Mike M knew about the head injury and asked to see the back of my head. He said it didn't look too bad, and he promised to take care of me and make sure I got well ASAP.

Mike M had a low, smoky voice, and sounded like he was a heavy smoker. As I was a smoker myself, most of the guys who approached me were smokers, too. There was something that bonded smokers. We became a minority, and as such, we tended to get together in small groups.

I drove, following Mike M's directions, and we arrived at a small restaurant not far away. The restaurant had a patio, and as the weather was beautiful that day, it was more than warm enough to sit outside in the garden. This was a significant achievement in rainy Seattle. The patio was full of women, some of them had their babies with them, and some of them were older women who sat in groups. Music was playing not too loudly, and I loved the tempo of the songs. All the songs were dance songs, and I could have started dancing right there. I moved my body to the beat but stopped when I saw that Mike M was looking at me and smiling. I was embarrassed a little, as I was caught off guard, but I smiled back. I felt my head getting heavy, and it meant that I needed to relax and let my body rest. I was recovering, I reminded myself. *Relax, you are not well.* It had been about a week since it all happened.

It was still early, almost five, and it was still in the middle of happy hour. Mike M urged me to order "whatever you feel like." I ordered a glass of red wine and a small salad. Mike M ordered a soda and a hamburger while flirting with the waitress. I loved the way he was so open and outgoing. Mike M chatted constantly, and it was the first time that I didn't have to lead the conversation or ask too many questions on a first date. I loved it, as it gave me the time to relax in my chair, sip my wine quietly, and enjoy the sun. I felt like a lizard and appreciated every second out there. My body needed the rest. The glass of wine knocked me down a little. Maybe I shouldn't have been drinking, but I couldn't resist a good glass of wine. Maybe some water would help, and I sipped a little from my water glass.

Suddenly, Mike M moved his chair back, took my hand, and pulled me up out of my chair. A quiet song, "How sweet it is to be loved by you," played over the speakers. Mike M danced with me, slowly while holding my body close to his. I loved it. I enjoyed dancing and always looked for a partner. Men usually were not into dancing, and it was rare to find a guy who would dance because he enjoyed it. It looked like Mike M enjoyed every second of it.

The song finished, and Mike M helped me to sit back down slowly, making sure to ask how I was feeling. Around us, everybody clapped their hands and smiled at us.

"Do you know how jealous all these women are right now?" Mike M whispered in my ear, smiling. He reminded me, for a second, of the cat from *Alice in Wonderland*.

"Why are you saying that?" I asked him, still a little dizzy from our dance.

"Look at them," he said. "They all look bored, and nobody is here with a man." I looked around again. He was right. I had noticed it as well when we came in. The patio was full of women, and all of them were now looking at us and smiling at me. I smiled back and thought, *if they only knew that I had just met this guy an hour ago*. I was sure their partners were at work, and I was sure that some of them were with their mothers, which I would love to do if my mother was still alive, but this was not the case. I was the only one there with a man, and he was literally spinning me around. The dance, the wine, the sun—my head was spinning from everything. Everybody had a story, and my story looked like it was the best one around at that moment, so I decided to enjoy my good luck and relax.

Mike M kept chatting and bouncing around, doing everything he could to make me smile and laugh. He asked questions about me, my family, my Israeli history. Since Mike M was a Marine, my service with the IDF, even though it was thirty years ago, made a big impression on him. He also found the moment and told me about the car he planned to buy. He liked fast cars.

Mike M tipped very generously when he paid the bill, and I saw the waitress smile when she came to pick the tab. I liked men who were good tippers because it meant something about the way they saw the world and how they treated other people.

My head felt weighty, and with the wine, it even became heavier. I needed to stand up and get out of the restaurant. I needed to walk around for a while. I told Mike M that I would wait for him outside, next to the car, as I wanted to smoke. Mike M asked me to wait for him, as he needed to visit the bathroom, and he made me promise that I would not start my cigarette without him. I promised. While Mike M was in the toilet, I had few minutes to roll myself a joint, and when he came back, I was ready for him, with a nice rolled cigarette in my hand.

"What is that?" Mike M asked me when I lit up my joint.

"Homemade smoke." I laughed. "Full of natural ingredients."

Mike M asked for a puff. "Are you sure?" I asked him. "Are you allowed to smoke weed?"

"Oh, hell," he said. "I'll be officially discharged in ten days, and I want to see who will tell me what to do now."

I shared my smoke, and I saw his eyes open wide at the first puff. He loved it! He calmed down and looked at me like he was about to hug me any minute.

I drove Mike M to his place, which was five minutes away. We arrived at a small apartment building, where Mike M rented an apartment on the first floor. Mike M invited me in for a glass of wine. I was dying to see his home, so I agreed. It was still early in the evening, sevenish, and the days were getting longer. It would take another hour, at least, for the sun to start going down.

I entered Mike M's place and looked around. It was clean, very rustic—the sofa was old, the carpet was raggedy, and there was no other furniture besides the couch. I did notice a file cabinet like what you see in old movies, made of metal, and it was taller than me. There was an inflatable kayak in the corner of the room, and a U.S. flag, folded in a triangle. I asked to use the restroom and entered a clean, spotless bathroom, where there was one toothbrush in the sink. A soldier's place, clean and impeccable.

The place had a balcony, which was one hundred feet from the Green River. I had the feeling I could jump from the patio and just run towards the water. But I was in no condition to do so.

The wine glass was already waiting for me on the balcony table when I came out. The small kitchen was spotless, although I saw dishes drying on the table next to the sink. It looked like somebody had recently cooked something.

We had a glass of wine and kept our discussion going. Mike M had gone through a lot in his career in the Marines and was very ready to become a civilian. But he was still thinking and talking as if he was in the Marines, which meant ordering and making decisions that only a commander would consider. He was such an alpha. Mike M was also a great kisser, and we finished our date with a long hot kiss, while he pushed me slowly back on the file cabinet, where I could rest my back. Oh, this is why you need a file cabinet. I giggled to myself, thinking of few more ways we could use the file cabinet. When I said I had to leave, Mike M made me promise to text him as soon as I got home.

Mike M had a very basic phone, and he explained to me that this was his way to avoid the NSA. I had no idea what he was talking about. Mike M had to tell me what NSA meant. I Googled it right away, of course, and I thought he was crazy.

"They" were after him because he knew too much, so every month he threw away his phone and bought a new one, he told me. Pre-paid. "The Mossad is in town," he said, and I tried to hide my chuckle. I kissed him on his forehead and said goodnight.

I had three text messages from him when I got back home. It was a thirty-minute drive. I was happy with the attention from him and texted back a goodnight message. "I got home, and everything is fine. Thank you for a lovely time."

The next morning, there was a greeting awaiting me, sent at six a.m. Mike M missed me already and wanted to know when we were meeting again. Mike M invited me to his place to take the kayak out on the water, and he promised he would cook lunch. He knew I was not working for the next week or so. I loved the idea, so I packed my swimming suit and announced to my kids that I would be back for dinner.

When I got there, it was exactly as I imagined. Mike M threw the kayak off the patio. We walked outside, picked it up, and carried it to the water fifty feet from us. The weather was still wonderful, and the river was quiet with a soft breeze in the air. I was very relaxed, which was a new feeling for me. Mike M was doing everything and ordered me to get into a "laid back" mode. I followed the order but reminded him that I was not his soldier. Mike M smiled and said, "If I had soldiers like you, I would never leave the Marines." We both laughed.

Mike M paddled, as I laid back and enjoyed the sun and the water splashing around me. The river took us slowly with Mike M's paddling. We got to a curve where we could see the beautiful big houses that were built to have the best view of the river.

Suddenly, we saw a huge black dog running toward us. It stopped at the water line and barked like crazy. It looked mad and mean. Although we were not close to it, and it didn't look like the dog was going to jump in the water and swim toward us, it still felt spooky. It ruined the atmosphere and our tranquility.

I saw Mike M's face getting red. "Fuck you," he yelled. Then Mike M shouted a few sentences, which turned into a whole story, but I had to ask him to repeat it because the dog wouldn't stop its loud and obnoxious barking.

Mike M kayaked often on the river, and that dog was always there when he passed the curve, barking and acting crazy. Mike M usually paddled downriver, while swearing at the dog. But today was going to be different.

Mike M stopped paddling but kept his paddle in the water, so the kayak would stay in the same spot. Mike M yelled back at the dog, as if it was a person, or the other way around when Mike M barked like a dog. It became a war of who was growling louder and with more aggression. It was hilarious. Mike M, at one point, was literally barking at the dog, with the dog responding with crying noises. After few minutes, the black dog started whimpering and ran away, with his tail tucked between his legs. The real alpha had won!

We looked at each other and burst into a massive laugh. I was literally crying! Mike M was very proud of himself and let loose with a Tarzan shout.

Mike M took fantastic care of me that day. I was not allowed to do anything, but relax and enjoy my time, while Mike M ran around, making lunch, serving, cleaning up after us, and asking me every ten minutes how I was feeling and how my head was. I was never taken care of that way, and I was very appreciative. We made out a little, but had to stop when my head started to hurt as the scalp around the stitches had begun to swell. Mike M made sure to stop the goofing around as soon as I mentioned my pain. He got me to a lying position, with a cushion under my head and an ice pack close to the stitches. Mike M did great.

I left for home that day, thinking that Mike M was the most incredible man in the world, gentle, thoughtful. Masculine, and he was a great cook.

We saw each other the next day as well, and it took ten minutes from the time I walked into his apartment to the minute we were on the living room carpet, ripping each other's clothes away. The guy was unstoppable. And so was I.

A couple of hours later, we relaxed and went to the kitchen to grab some food and water. We sat on the patio watching the river, and I was still blushing from our recent exercises. I was not expecting that kind of welcome, and it was one I thought I could repeat again if I could just finish my glass of water. But my head was not agreeing with me, and I found myself in Mike M's bed, falling asleep. He let me sleep until I woke up a couple of hours later. He told me that he kept checking on me all this time, tucking me in with the sheet and making sure my breathing was healthy, and I didn't vomit. A soldier and a caring lover. How lucky can one get?

Mike M had three kids. Two boys and one daughter, Rebecca. The folded flag was there because one of his boys had died in Iraq. The other son was in the Marines as well, and Rebecca was an FBI agent. A very patriotic family, who talked the talk and walked the walk. I always admired people like that.

Going out with Mike M or being in the same room with him felt like there was a gorilla in the room. A gentle one that was under control, but still a gorilla. Kind of a King Kong. His masculinity was all over the place, and if other men were around, they physically became smaller next to Mike M. Although Mike M was not a tall man, he looked and sounded like one.

We said goodnight at an early hour. I felt in need of my bed and my place, and we promised each other we would meet the next day, Saturday, but I had forgotten about my brunch date with Mike S.

When I got home, I had three text messages from Mike M.

I made myself a cup of tea and texted back Mike M, thanking him for a letting me fall asleep, and for taking such a good care of me in other departments.

Mike M's answer was very immediate."What took you so long to answer me? I am sitting here worried about you and waiting to hear from you!" I assured Mike M that I was okay and safe at home, and again, thanked him for his concern. I also mentioned that I couldn't meet with him as planned for breakfast, but I could see him later that day. Mike M's answer came very quickly. "I hope you are not seeing anybody else." I answered him back. "I am free tomorrow for dinner. Do you want to see me or not?" Mike M agreed.

The next morning I got myself ready to meet Mike S. It was a great Seattle summer morning, and I wore a summery skirt and a sleeveless blouse. I had the look of a "Sexy Mama," or at least this is what my daughters told me, and off I went to meet Mike Security.

I parked my car and saw a gigantic man, wearing: a jersey shirt with the local football team logo for the Seattle Seahawks, shorts, socks, and huge sports shoes. This was a very local dress up for a weekend breakfast in Seattle. Most locals even wore this outfit to work on Fridays. I was always amused to see guys coming to work in shorts, socks, and sandals. Nothing was too ugly to wear, which made everything acceptable and kind of fun.

While I parked the car, the giant man walked toward me. He took every step very seriously, but his face was wide open with a large smile. He had beautiful green eyes and a beard that suited him perfectly. Not a skinny guy, but not heavy, either. And tall! OMG, people were looking at him while he walked, as he was so tall.

I got out of my car and stepped on the sidewalk next to my car. The sidewalk provided five more inches to my height, so when Mike S finally approached me, I was not so short next to him, and could—almost—look him at the neck level.

Mike S hugged me right away. I pushed him back gently, and said, "You are not as tall as I thought." We both started laughing, and I stepped down to the road, and I was on the same level where he stood. I looked at Mike S and again started laughing. I was at the same height as his belly button. This was going to be a comic date, I thought.

Issaquah Cafe is a diner that served only breakfast and lunch. Big substantial breakfasts and lunches. I was not aware of their portion size, so ordered the California Benedict—love love love Benedict style eggs—and when the waitress asked me about the kind of bread and pancakes I wanted with it, I just told her to bring everything she had. Mike S ordered a bacon omelet. I had seen Mike S hiding a smile when I had given my order. After the waitress left, I asked Mike S the reason for his smile. He asked me if I had visited the Issaquah Cafe before, and I admitted that I had not. He smiled again and said that I was about to have a big surprise. It sounded like I was about to have a tasty treat. That was what I understood.

When the food arrived, I understood what Mike S meant. Literally. Everything was big, and my last comment "bring it all" made it even worse. The table was covered with food, and Mike S was just sitting there, smiling and looking at me.

"Now, honey, you have to eat it all," he said, looking amused.

"Now honey," I said, "we have leftovers for the coming year." We both laughed and started to dig into all that food. Well, quality and quantity do not always go together, and I found myself very quickly taking a piece of toast and jam, and pushing away the food plate. It was too greasy for my taste, and I needed a light diet that would not make me stuffed, as had happened with my injury, it just made me fall asleep on the spot. I usually didn't visit diners of this kind, as I had been used to a Mediteranian diet for years.

Mike S asked about my head condition, and I told him that I still felt dizzy sometimes mainly when I ate breakfast with a handsome man. He loved my answer and assured me he was wobbly as well.

We finished breakfast and went for a walk to a pond nearby. There were benches along the walking path. We found a seat that was somehow private but still exposed to any person who walked on the trail. We sat down and turned to each other and started a kiss. It was spontaneous, and it felt amazing. Mike S was a great kisser, and his vast body just wrapped me, the petite one, into his, and I felt I was, literally, in good hands.

We finished the long kiss, and became aware of people looking at us. We were not so hidden as we thought we were. Another burst of a laughter. We held hands and continued to talk. Mike S had a very demanding job. He was part of an individual department that was established, after 9/11 events, and he was very dedicated to his career and his country.

Another patriotic guy. How did I get all of them? I guessed my IDF experience made them curious and attracted them to me in the first place, and they felt they could share with me things that other women would not understand. They were both right—Mike M and Mike S—and they both admitted it later. I was able to listen to their stories, understand the pressure and the circumstances that they were acting under and provide a different view when needed. I thanked my IDF service and the time I lived in Israel, not for the first time in my life. It took me far in my online dating life as well.

Mike S and I said goodbye for the day, and scheduled our next date for a week later, as Mike S was working shifts that changed every few weeks. I was very eager to see Mike S again. He was an alpha man but, compared to Mike M, he was quiet, and being in his presence was tranquilizing and made me relaxed.

Later that day, I met Mike M for dinner. He cooked pizza Marine style. The Marine style meant that the dough was "opened" or rolled with a wine bottle and the tomato sauce was fire hot! But, as one who was raised in the Middle East, this was a piece of cake for me, and Mike M thought it was very impressive.

"Wait until you taste my Polish recipes," I told him.

"Hotter than this sauce?" he asked me.

"Kind of." I laughed thinking about the stuffed sweet fish, Gefilte fish, we eat for the Jewish New Year, Rosh Hashana, to which we add a fire hot horseradish. If you are not raised on this kind of food, you will most probably spit it out after the first bite, if brave enough to try it. As they say, it is an acquired taste.

We had dessert in bed. Mike M remembered I had said I loved vanilla/rum/raisin ice cream, and he went out of his way to find some. I knew it was not an easy task and appreciated it very much. Mike M also used the ice cream to show me how much he enjoyed my body and just asked me to relax and be there. I followed his instructions, and we found ourselves sweaty and falling asleep two hours later. Mike M had not come even one time, while I was breathless and stopped counting my orgasms after the fourth one.

When I opened my eyes, it was nine p.m., and Mike M was standing naked, next to his closet, with a bottle of vodka in his hand and a bottle of pills in the other. I asked him if he was okay, and Mike M smiled at me and assured me that he had never felt better. He still had an enormous erection and looked very sexy just standing there. I was worried about the alcohol and asked him why he was hiding his drinking from me.

"Do you have any alcohol issues?" I asked.

Mike M promised me he did not that he just felt like a shot of vodka to cool down, as I was making his blood go too fast. He came back to bed and went down under the covers. I did not oppose.

In the next week, our dates became daily, and we spent a lot of time together. Mike M was about to leave for Washington D.C. for his final discharge ceremony and asked me to join him. He said he would cover all the expenses, and we could stay for another day and tour the city.

I have to admit that I was very eager to join him. It sounded like an adventure, and I had never been to D.C. before. I also had time off from work, recovering from my injury, so no problem in this area as well.

Only one thing bothered me. I had asked Mike M to check with his daughter, Rebecca, who would be there as well. I wanted to make sure this whole plan was okay with her. I didn't want to surprise her with my presence and thought it would be a respectful thing to ask for her permission.

Mike M dismissed this idea and said she would be just fine with me coming with him. He had already told her about me, and she was thrilled that her father had found a woman who could handle him. Hmm, already told his daughter about me. This was a little early in the game for me, but who was I to judge. Rebecca told her father that he better treat me right. Otherwise, she would take care of him. I laughed when I heard that, and Mike M complained that now he had two women in his life that he needed to answer to.

I raised my concern again, just to confirm Rebecca accepted my presence. This whole situation was somehow surreal. There was no rationale for me flying to Washington D.C. with a man I had met less than two weeks before, as his girlfriend, to participate in an official honorable discharge. He was a general in the Marines, and the planned ceremony was going to be a huge deal. The other huge deal was the fact that Rebecca, his twenty-six year-old daughter would be there as well. His son was in active service on a different continent and could not make it.

I did not want to be in the middle of a family drama. I could deal with a U.S. Marine General, but I did not want to deal with an upset daughter. I had two of them, and I always made sure that I was fair and sincere with my actions if it might impact them.

Mike M assured me that she would be fine, and got me on the floor for another round of "let me take care of you, baby" as he loved to call it.

Mike M suggested we fly to San Francisco when we returned from Washington D.C. He asked me if I wanted to make some quick money, as I was complaining about the high mortgage I was paying every month. Mike M knew a club where live sex shows were presented on a central stage—sort of a big glass capsule, where the audience stood in a circle watching. Nobody could touch the couple in the capsule. The couple on stage wore masks, so they would not be recognized, but other than that everything was real. They paid three thousand dollars for one act per night and were always looking for new people. With my body and the way we were having sex, we could get even more money. Mike M offered to drop his share so I could take all the money. Cash. I was shocked. I pushed him away immediately, stood up, and told him that I was done. My sex life was mine and was not to be shared or used to entertain anybody. To my surprise, Mike M had a huge smile on his face. I almost kicked him."Why are you smiling? What is wrong with you?"

Mike M used to swear a lot, and I begged him to stop when he was with me. I could not hear anymore fuck/shit/stupid and so on. Mike M had done very well since I had asked him, and now he looked at me, smiled and said, "You are a fucking good woman. I want you to be my wife."

I laughed and assured him that this would not happen and asked him again to stop swearing. He said he was testing me, and I passed the test. I asked Mike M not to do it again. I preferred open and honest discussions and not stupid tests. But this was what he knew—tests. He was tested in the Marines all the time. Talking was overrated, actions spoke. I reminded him he wasn't in the Marines anymore, and I was not his soldier. I was a very straightforward person and would not lie to make somebody happy. We agreed that this was how we would continue our discussions in the future and both of us would be honest.

In the meantime, I had a chance to see Mike S for a couple of dinners and a stormy two hours in his car after one of them. I loved his size and his temperament. He never got mad or upset and always knew what to say to calm me down or anybody else who was around. Just the opposite from Mike M, who would take any opportunity to get into an argument, for any stupid reason. A real King Kong. I was always on guard with Mike M when we went out, making sure he was not upset with any guy who was too nice to me, or if he thought that somebody was not nice enough to me. I could not win with him.

Mike M sent me texts ten times a day, for no reason, just to ask me what I was doing and what I had had for lunch. It was summertime, and Mike M had a whole month off until the school year started. I started to get annoyed.

It was a Friday night, and I was on my way to Mike M's. We planned to go out for dinner and drinks and find a club that had some good music. Mike M was a great dancer and shared it with me on a few occasions already, including his living room. He would play all kinds of music, and get me to dance with him. I loved that about him. Mike S, on the other hand, used to sit at the bar and watch me dance by myself until a slow dance came on, and then he would join me. It was funny to dance with him, as my head and his belly button were on the same height. I loved to go crazy when I danced, but he was a big guy and a serious one, except in the bedroom, where he let himself go.

When Mike M opened the door, he had only a towel on his hips. Mike M was sixty years old and was shaped like a twenty-five-year old man. His service in the Marines kept him fit, and although he was a heavy smoker, he exercised on a daily basis and made sure to stay in shape. The towel was a little raised. He had a beautiful massive erection under it. I smiled and let him take me to the living room, where he managed to take off half of my clothes in two seconds. He knew his job well. Mike M started by giving me a long deep massage, precisely what I needed after almost a whole week at work and before the weekend. I had gone back to work three days before my sick days were done. I had a critical project going on and my injury had put me behind. I felt much better, but the long hours had taken their toll, and I was all stressed. Mike M knew how to get my body to relax. It was not a sexual massage, although I knew I could turn it around any moment if I wanted to. For God's sake, the man was wearing only a towel. Suddenly

I thought, wait a second. Something here was wrong. All these times we had spent together, Mike M had not had even one orgasm, and was always able to go on for hours. Had that been a viagra bottle he was holding with the vodka? Oh well, he was a big boy, and if that was what worked for him, good for him. It worked very well for me. I closed my eyes and tried to relax.

At one point, while massaging my back, Mike M started to talk about the trip to D.C. and me joining him. The ceremony was to take place in four days, and he was still waiting for my answer to buy me a ticket. He repeated his offer to pay for everything and to stay another day so I could tour the city. He knew D.C. very well.

I reminded Mike M, quietly, that he was supposed to talk to his daughter, Rebecca, and get her blessing for my arrival.

Mike M stopped massaging me immediately. We were on the sofa, and he went from a relaxed sitting position on my butt and rubbing my back, to a sitting position on the couch, next to my legs, his hands joined together on his chest, and the erection still protruded under the towel. He looked agitated, and I thought he looked like the grumpy dwarf from Snow White. My mind worked weirdly sometimes.

Mike M yelled at me and told me that this was not Rebecca's business, and neither Rebecca nor I would tell him what to do. He wanted me to come with him, and this was what was going to happen.

I brought myself to a sitting position as well, but still with my legs on the sofa. "So, you did not talk to Rebecca, did you?" I asked.

"No, and it's not any of her goddam business," was Mike M's answer.

I got up very slowly and looked at him. "Mike, you understand I will not be able to join you, unless Rebecca gives her blessing, right?"

"Do not tell me how to run my life!" Mike M shouted at me repeatedly.

I got up from the sofa and got dressed. Once I was done, I sat next to the dining table and rolled myself a joint. All this time, Mike M was swearing and cursing about the situation, how nobody would tell him what to do. I stood up and headed for the door. His last sentence to me was, "If you leave now, you will never come back." I looked at Mike M, didn't say a word, and left the place.

My ride home was quiet. I was sad, but I knew I had done the right thing. Mike M was not an easy-going person, and drama was an integral part of his life. I wanted a fun non-dramatic life, and with Mike M it would never happen.

I woke up in the morning and found three emails from Mike M in my private Gmail inbox.

In the first email he called me names, and whore was one of them.

In the second email, he blamed me for running away from him at a time when I was needed.

In the third email, Mike M found more hard words to add to my behavior.

I wrote him an email back. "We both have daughters, and none of us would like to see somebody treating our girls the way you are treating me right now. Please stop and take a look at your actions."

Mike M answered with more cursing and "fuck you, bitch" wishes. I blocked him both on my Gmail and on my phone, as the same messages would probably come in as texts as well. I also made sure to block him, immediately, on the online dating site.

I had a date with Mike Security the next day. I really liked Mike S, and I knew he enjoyed my company as well. Mike S had mentioned something about being exclusive. And he was suspicious of me seeing another guy other than him. I knew that he was seeing other women, and I felt weird about it. It was very early in the game, but it was a game that was played fast. Mike S was still living at home with his ex-wife but was about to move to a rental in two weeks. At that time, we kept meeting for different events, like a late drink on his way back from work at eleven or dinner in a local place, and we always ended the date with a hot get together in the back of his big truck. I never made out in a car before, and I felt like a sixteen-year-old while doing it. I really liked that man.

The minute I met Mike S for dinner the next day, my phone started vibrating with text messages. The messages were coming from an unknown number, and I didn't know what was happening. The notes were one or two words, one of them was bitch, the other whore. My phone was on the table, and Mike S saw one of the notes and my face. I was angry and pissed like crazy.

Mike Marine must have replaced his phone and was texting me from the new number. I had to tell Mike S the story and block the new number.

Dinner was weird. I told a short version of Mike M's story, dropping the fantastic sex and the spotless home parts. Mike S knew guys like Mike M, so he was not shocked by my story. The only part that he was interested in was the fact that I had left his place, and I was done with Mike M.

Mike S wanted exclusivity, and that was a great moment for him to ask for it. I reminded Mike S that he was still living with his ex, and his divorce wouldn't be final for two months. I didn't want to be Mike S's rebound. Mike S promised me that this was not the case, and I decided to believe him. I was not looking to get married, but I was looking for one partner, and I thought that Mike S was perfect.

We both agreed that we would drop whoever we were in touch with at that time and enjoy our time together whenever we wanted.

This decision made me invite Mike S for brunch, at my place, and I asked my kids to join. Mike S was very respectful and knew how to treat people. I knew he would do just fine with my kids. My daughters, on the other hand, decided that they didn't want to meet Mike S, and each of them arranged for a sleepover the night before. It was their decision, and I respected it.

I still wanted to continue with the brunch plan with Mike S at my house. I was tired of eating out, and Mike S insisted on paying for everything all the time. I did not feel right about it. Mike S was making less money than me, but I didn't share this info with him. Usually, men hated the fact I made more money than them, and I saved this info for myself.

I was happy to cook for Mike S, and we had brunch outside on the deck among all the trees. I lived on top of a mountain and had an acre to myself. Mike S loved the place and complimented me on my cooking skills, even though I knew he was suffering. Mike S was a bacon and beans man. I cooked a shakshuka, which is a favorite Israeli dish of stewed tomatoes and poached eggs, traditionally spicy. It was a North African dish from Libya or Tunisia. But he kept on eating and complimenting my cooking. My phone rang, and I reached out and answered the call, without looking at the screen. I thought one of my girls probably needed something.

A spurt of cursing and yelling hit my ears. I was so surprised and shocked that I just dropped the phone on the table, while the screaming kept going. It was Mike M at eleven on Saturday morning, and he sounded drunk.

Mike S looked at me and asked me if he could take the phone and talk to the General. I nodded my head and did not say a word. I was shocked and embarrassed. I was also afraid and worried. Mike M knew my last name, and it was not hard to find my address. I did not want any drama coming to my house.

Mike S picked up the phone and calmly asked if he could help. Mike M continued to yell and asked him to put me on the call. Mike S told him that I was not interested in talking to him.

"Who are you?" Mike M barked at him. Mike S introduced himself as a good friend, and also mentioned the fact that he was part of the security forces. Mike S asked Mike M to stop calling, as the next time he called, it would be reported to the police as harassment and as a threat. Mike S added, in a very soft voice, "Buddy, go take a cold shower. It will help you feel better, and get off the booze."

Mike M ended the call and Mike Security looked at me, nodded his head, and said, "I smell trouble coming with you."

I just hugged him and gave him a kiss. Trouble was my second name.

Mike Security and I lasted together for another two months. We were sitting in a cinema when Mike S fell asleep and snored for the whole movie. On the way home, Mike S confessed that he was tired and couldn't keep up with my energy. Mike S was not a fifty-six-year old man. He was a sixty-two and had been lying about his age. I wished him all the best, and I will always cherish some of the memories from him, but I'm not sharing which.

13 - MIKE #77

There was Mike #76, and a day later Mike #77, who was a product of an Equatorial mother and a French father. He was funny, spoke French, and drank wine like a Frenchman. He had a box of white wine in his refrigerator and treated it like a bottle of mineral water in the few hours I spent at his place. But I'm getting ahead of myself here.

Mike #77 was three years younger than me, carried a few extra pounds, sported a lousy haircut, and showed up for our first date wearing shorts, sandals, and socks—the Seattle formal dress code. Very sexy, I know. Every time I saw these guys I wanted to cry for help! Why God, why? So NOT sexy!

I took Mike #77 on our first date to the Blue Moon Tavern. I loved the place and had gone there frequently a couple of months earlier with Mike #70. I knew that Mike #70 left before 7 p.m., so it was safe for me to step in. Mike #77 had grown up about five miles away from the bar, but he had never visited it before.

"How come?" I asked. "Did you ever hear about this place, when you lived in this area?"

"Oh yes," was his answer. "But I never took the time."

I guess that this is what happens when you live close to an attraction; you just don't take the time to visit it as a tourist would because it's just a part of the view.

The next week, Mike #77 invited me for dinner at his place for baked salmon, cooked veggies, and lots of white wine. Mike #77 had just divorced and had a nine-year-old daughter who stayed with her mother.

We finished our dinner, and Mike #77 offered me some of his pot. Seattle is a green city, one of the first cities in the States that made recreational marijuana legal. We enjoyed his weed; I smoked a little, and he smoked a lot. Mike #77's next suggestion was to visit his local bar, a five-minute walk from his place. I had shared with him my bar, and now he wanted to share with me his bar. I liked the idea.

The place was big and noisy with a lot of pool tables. Mike #77 ordered beer for both of us and showed off his billiard skills. He was a good player. I knew nothing about the game, but I loved to learn to play from pro guys. It had its unique touches, and it was very erotic to have my own instructor. The teaching required my mentor to stand behind me and help me with the moves. I let Mike #77 make all the necessary moves behind me, and we both enjoyed those sweet minutes. I even made some good shots and was excited about my latest achievement.

Once I started hitting the balls by myself, and my back was turned to Mike #77, I noted that my beer glass was emptying very quickly without me touching it. In the beginning, I didn't notice it, but when I reached out for my beer after hitting a ball, I couldn't find the beer where I had left it. When I did see it, it was almost empty. Mike #77 was drinking both of our drinks. I looked at Mike #77, who was laughing and thought it was a good joke. I didn't think it was funny, so I went and got myself a new beer and asked him not to touch it. Five minutes later, my beer was gone again.

That was it; I was done there. I told him, "Let's go back to your place. I need to pick up my stuff."

We went back to his place, a friendly first-floor rental, with a patio viewing a green belt. We sat there quietly enjoying the peaceful moment, having another glass of wine and smoke. Suddenly Mike #77 started talking. Let me remind you, it's our second date.

"I think you are a fantastic woman, but you have to stop smoking pot so much," he said. "I really want you to be healthy. It's good that you are going to the gym because you need to lose a few pounds."

I smiled softly in the dark. How sweet, right? He cared about me. I choked a bit, and he continued talking. I wasn't listening, as my mind was telling me I was too drunk to drive, which meant I needed to stay for a sleepover. I just wanted to go to sleep.

He was happy when I suggested moving to the bedroom, and he started messing around right away. Well, guys, after two beers of your own, two beers of your dates, and about ten glasses of wine, things don't work as they should, unless you are twenty-five.

So, he tried a new technique to be funny, I guess. Butterfly on the stomach, which I hate. When Mike #77 did it the first time, I asked him to stop and told him I hated it. When he did it for the second time, I grabbed his whole head firmly and held it between my hands and looked him in the eyes and repeated my statement. "I hate it. Please don't do it again, it is not a good feeling for me, and I really don't like it."

On the third time, I got out of bed and started to get dressed.

"What are you doing?" he yelled at me.

"I'm going home," I said. It was three in the morning, and I had a forty-minute drive and a dog that needed to go out in the morning. Oh, and I had a third date with Mike #80 later that day. We were going to the Polish Festival, so I knew I needed some sleep before I drove there.

Mike #77 grabbed my hand, and begged, in English, French, and Spanish, for me not to leave, promising he would never do it again.

I stopped getting dressed and went back to bed. We both fell asleep in two seconds. I woke up at six in the morning and got dressed quietly. I was almost ready to leave when Mike #77 woke up and looked at me. "Where are you going?" he asked. "I was planning on making you breakfast." I thanked him, kissed him on his forehead, and explained that I had not planned to stay, and I hadn't brought anything with me. Besides, I had a dog waiting for me at home.

Mike #77 was very disappointed, but he got out of bed and walked me to the door. He promised he would be in touch. He made me promise I would be in touch as well. At that moment, I would have guaranteed anything, as long as he opened the door and let me out.

I drove home, went to sleep, and met Mike #80 four hours later at the Polish Festival.

It took Mike #77 three days to text me a message, in French. "I beg you, please call me."

It was amusing and romantic to see it. I texted back a happy face and wished Mike #77 all the best. But I did not think that we were a match. He texted back and asked me if he could call me. I said yes. The phone rang immediately.

Mike #77 was funny and charming as usual. He moved between languages, and he used all the right words to impress. I laughed and enjoyed the conversation and told him he was a great guy, but he wasn't for me. He had a nine-year-old daughter and was going through a lot of drama as the divorce process had just began, and he was struggling financially as a result. I had older kids, no drama, and could afford to go out and enjoy activities with no stress.

"That's it?" he asked. "Anything else that is in our way?"

"You really want the whole truth and nothing but the truth?" I love this phrase.

He did.

"I warn you," I said, "you don't know me, I'm not from here, and the rules of politically correct are not something I follow or even feel apply to me."

Mike #77 laughed and said that he had been raised by parents who weren't from this country so I wouldn't surprise him.

"Okay, "I said, "you asked for it. You have a drinking problem, which impacts your sex abilities. You are overweight and look older than your age You are not in shape and don't do anything to be in one. You dress awful, your financial situation sucks, and it will take you a long time and a lot of drama to get out of it. You have been fired from your job, and now you are a contractor who works crazy shift hours for Boeing, and this will not change shortly."

There was silence on the line. Mike #77 thanked me for my input and wished me all the best. I wished him the same as well.

The next time Mike #77 texted me, it was six months later. He complained that I had entered his life as a storm and vanished as one. He wanted to see me again. I thanked him for his interest and said that I was involved in a relationship and very happy where I was. He kept texting, saying that he would like to do standup with me, and he would pay for my beer and would not touch it.

I blocked him on my phone.

14 - #80 FOREVER

I was tired. Frustrated from all the men who reached out to me, asking to meet me, and spending endless dates listening to guys whining about their past relationships over drinks, and me, wanting to get out of there as soon as possible as the conversation turned to terrible and or ended up being dull. I wanted to meet somebody who I could talk to for hours, who would make me laugh and cry and who would teach me something new—all the time. Intelligence was always my primary attraction when it came to men, or maybe I should say, intellectual men. People who loved to learn new things, were open to the world, and enjoyed new cultures. No judgment and no small talk for me. Mister, can we skip all the BS right away and move into an interesting discussion, about the world, and geography? I wanted to know where he had traveled recently and what he liked about it. I wanted to know where and what he wanted to see next. I wanted to ask a man about the next comedy show coming to town and ask him to join me.

In my frustration, I decided to try a new approach for a new online profile on the dating sites. My idea for a new profile included a photograph of an ear. That was all.

And I did. I wrote a new profile explaining why I was doing it and answering—again-- all the questions that OKCupid had on its site. This time I was bold, and I didn't hesitate to answer questions that I had skipped before. I also added many comments to any questions that got my attention.

Question: *Did you join OKCupid just so you could find people to have sex with?*
My answer: *No, but if it happens, it is okay.*

I looked for men's responses to the question, **What's worse on a first date?**
No physical attraction
Nothing to talk about

All the male profiles I saw answered "physical attraction." That's BS. BS because you can have an attraction for the first ten minutes, and after another five minutes of discussion, you just want to run away from there, either one of you.

I wrote a new profile and posted it out there. I thought I was so smart, playing the best game of my life. I felt strong, sturdy, and was full of myself. This time I was going to find the right guy. The one whose hand I would hold when we went out, the one who I would be proud to introduce to my friends, and he would be so smart that I would just want to listen to what he had to say every time he opened his mouth. Yes, I wanted to be the small little woman, who took care of her man and enjoyed doing it. I had more than enough running around and breaking the record of "how many dates I could squeeze in during a day."

My New "Ear" Profile

"I noticed that instead of reading my profile, men just see my pics and send me a "hi" ...I'm trying to change it :) So only one pic here. And no face. To keep it even more interesting. It is also supposed to be a funny and sexy self-presentation.

SO, if you don't share the same sense of humor, and you are "suspicious," please skip this profile and save me from your comments.

I'm a "Joan Rivers" type. If you can't handle this kind of humor, you will not enjoy my company. If you do enjoy Joan Rivers, you will laugh a lot.

OKCupid would not let me put Dolly Parton's picture on my profiled, but... Yes, I look very much like Dolly, and yes, I'm referring to the curves.

Please continue reading, and if you like what you read, please get in touch, and we will take it from there.

I appreciate a profile with more than one picture, and photos where your face is seen clearly.

Yes, I am forty-eight, I live in Seattle, and I'm a real blond (hair only).

I'm a career woman and the mother of two grown children who live away from home.

Originally from Europe, I've been here for the past fifteen years, and I'm doing very well in my position.

I'm fun, witty, enjoy interesting discussions, have a crazy sense of humor, and love to engage people around me with my husky laugh.

I have an accent and people usually approach me with questions about it. I have been told it is very sexy. Men still turn their heads when I pass them, and young studs are knocking on my door. Not interested. I'm looking to have fun, but with a real man and with only one man.

I love the outdoors, short hikes, beaches, lakes. I enjoy attending wine tastings, going out, listening to live music, visiting farmers' markets, eating, having picnics anywhere. I'm a great cook. I love taking road trips, spending long weekends away, dancing, and the list goes on.

Sex is significant to me, and your touch and smell are part of it. I love to feel my man, kiss him, hold hands, and make out whenever possible. I love to give and get and enjoy a gentle and rough touch. I'm not into crazy stuff, but I know that with the right man things can go wild.

Here is what I think I'm looking for.

I don't care how you look and where you come from, as long as you currently live in the Seattle area.

You must be smart. You have to be. It all starts up there. For me.

You must have a great sense of humor and love to laugh.

You have identified mutual interests in the list above (No...hunting and fishing are not included).

You love sex. You know you need an unusual partner to have a GREAT sex life, which means intimacy.

One-night stands are not my glass of wine/beer/whatever.

You want to take care of your woman—it's your passion whether outside or inside of the bedroom.

And last, but not least, you must have the budget to enjoy life.

I am not a "gold digger," but I do want to feel I'm taken care of, spoiled, cared for, and loved. If I get to feel all of these, you will be the happiest man in the world, I can assure you that.

It's not about expensive things; it is about doing things together and being able to enjoy the beautiful things in life as well...and, by the way, I love camping more than five-star hotels.

That's it for now. I'm sure I will be adding some more juicy details along the way.

May we all find our happy spot.

What I'm doing with my life

Besides work, which I enjoy very much—but not going to chat about it here—I'm looking for new and fun things to do, such as attending comedy shows, dance clubs, live music events in small towns. I love to invent new dishes and sharing a great wine with some good friends.

I'm really good at:

It's a long, long list, so let's say I'm good at many things that I believe are trivial, and other things where I excel and aren't so trivial.

Favorite food, books, movies, shows, music

Food - Spicy. Indian, Thai, small ethnic places, Mexican ONLY IF IT IS GOOD... Fine dining is nice sometimes. Love to cook. Love to cook with a partner. Love to cook with a partner who knows what's cooking :)

Books - usually about business or personal development.

Music - R&B for dancing. Light Jazz is friendly, Rock & Roll is always fun, classical can be entertaining as well. Got to know some Indie stuff lately. Learning from my kids.

Movies - if they have a message, real stories, if they make you think or laugh really hard. Hebrew Hammer anybody there? This is my kind of "make me laugh" movie.

Think Joan Rivers... with an accent :) that's me. Oh... and with Dolly's curves...

The six things I could never do without it

One thing I learned... there is nothing I could never do without. And it was a valuable lesson.

Okay ... seriously, besides food, water, kids, and all these essential things:

Health - very basic, but it is the most important. Sorry. Had to.

Lover's Touch - I need it physically:) and emotionally
Books/good conversations
Friends - especially GFs.
WINE - oh yeah
Music

I spend a lot of time thinking about

How come there are no real men around me? Is there something wrong with the water in the Seattle area? If I don't go clubbing, is online the only way to meet YOU? If I have an accent, does it mean that I can say whatever I want, as people usually don't ask if they don't understand?

On a typical Friday night, I am

No typical Friday:) I can decide to do something in the next hour and just go and do it... Dancing, wine tasting, listening to live music, taking a road trip, or staying at home and enjoying a quiet evening with myself as I have not found YOU yet!

You should message me if

you have read my profile... I suggest a couple of times...
you like it, are intrigued and would like to learn more.
you loved it, were intrigued and JUST HAVE to know more.
you think you are amazing and want to share it with the right woman!
and you have a crazy sense of humor... all day every day.

I was ready to meet Mr. Right and be only with him. I was also prepared for some new adventures, but this time I thought I had found a good filter. If you don't know how I look, and you still decide to approach me, you must be different.

Things did not go so well in the beginning. A lot of men approached me, complaining about the fact that I had no pictures. They called me in different names, starting with phony, fake, BS woman, and other nasty words, which made me feel bad for a second, and then I blocked them from my profile. The OKCupid site admininistrators even deleted my profile once because a few users had complained about my profile and not allowing me to post Dolly Parton's picture as my profile picture. My ear picture also received some bad reviews. I decided to ignore them all and just kept with my business, hoping to bump into a guy who would enjoy and embrace my experiment and would cooperate with me to the point that we would meet and greet. I was not going to respond to anybody who I didn't feel excellent about from the first minute. With all the questions and answers I filled up on the OKCupid site, I watched the percentage of OKCupid matches go up to eighty percent and higher, just to see if their logarithm worked. This meant that the other side had to answer at least nine hundred questions. I was very serious about it.

I was found by ex-dates, who knew me by my real profile and my life story. They didn't have good things to say, and I had to block some of them and explain to others that this was not about them—this was about me and my life, and they had nothing to say or complain about. It really felt weird to get their responses, as I was not committed to any of them, and I hadn't broken any understandings we had because we had nothing going on, right? But I guess they thought and felt differently.

I received a lot of hits from young men—and by young, I mean twenty-one-years old. These young men were sure that they were the answer to my prayers. Their messages always made me laugh, as my oldest daughter was around that age at that time, and I could not imagine her face if she saw me with a young guy her age.

One of these young men was very intriguing. He had a beautiful picture, had just turned twenty-four, owned his own restaurant, and sounded like he had a brain. I agreed to meet him. He was mature for his age and had a great life story. He used to work for a company full of women who identified his potential. He did not drink and was a very handsome guy, who knew how to dance, dress up, and have a conversation. He used to go out with few of those women to different events, and he provided various services. They loved him and supported him financially, until the point that he had saved enough money, and decided to leave his job and start his own business. He did not like to date young girls in his age range, as he felt that they were not independent, and many were very small-minded. Mike #78 had had a taste of older women, and he loved it. Mike #78 said that there was no way he could have gone back.

We had our first date on a sweltering summer evening. The only thing that mattered to me was to meet with him in a place that had air-conditioning. I learned quickly that most of the restaurants and bars in Seattle do not have air conditioning even installed in the place. We ended up changing the meeting location—I did—three times, as I was calling places to ask about air conditioning. The last place I called to ask this question, I told the waiter, who answered my call, that I was taking his name, and in case there was no air conditioning in place as he promised, I would hunt him down. I meant every word I said. His laugh was a little shivering while he kept assuring me that the place was cold enough.

Twenty-four-year old Mike #78 was a very short guy and was not dressed so sharp when we met. He apologized, explaining that this was his first evening off after working the whole month every day for the whole day. Mike #78 just opened his place—a Mexican restaurant in Kent—and was doing all he could to run it with as few workers as possible. I very much understood and assured him that he looked great, and I admired his passion and hard work.

Mike #78 didn't like the fact that I drank and smoked weed so much, which I usually do, when I am bored on a date. The next day, he sent me a long text message, explaining to me that he couldn't date me again for two reasons. I smoked too much weed, and I drank too much alcohol. I laughed so hard when I saw this text message. It was hilarious. A twenty-four-year old guy was preaching to me, the forty-eight-year old woman, about my smoking and drinking habits. I was thinking about myself at his age, and how I worked three jobs and was providing for my household, as my husband at that time was not doing very well financially. "Oh, Jesus," I thought. "I wish I had a husband like you twenty-four years ago! I thanked Mike #78 for his concern, wished him all the luck in the world, and said goodbye.

It was a sweltering summer in Seattle, and the evenings at home were not pleasant. I took advantage of any reason to get out and do something, and not stay at home and feel the sweat running through every pore on my body. I even went to see a movie with my daughter, a thing I usually don't do. I am not a fan of the smell of popcorn and being quiet for two hours. I do not even remember which movie it was, as most of the time, I just enjoyed the breeze in the cinema and thought about when the film ended and having to go home to sleep and sweat some more. I took three showers a day and a middle of the night shower was becoming a must during that time.

I kept getting more and more messages to my no-picture profile, and I finally found two guys who interested me. One had a very relaxed and hip picture, standing next to a hardcore motorcycle—this was Mike #79. The other one had a very nerdy image, with a big smile, which was Mike #80. Mike #79 and I had a ninety percent match. Mike #80 and I had a ninety-four percent match. I pretty much believed in these numbers, and the high percentage was a good sign, although I was not very happy with any of the pictures. No, I did not like motorcycles, and I did not feel safe on them. But Mike #79 sounded really fun, and we shared some mutual interests, such as music and a few other things. He also had his own motorcycle shop, which meant he was a business owner. I always appreciated business owners because there was a lot of work and thought behind running a business. I also kept in mind that business owners work crazy hours, and vacation was usually not on their calendar. But it was very early in the game, and

I really wanted to meet the guy who had a ninety percent match with me. We were planning to meet the next day, but then his store was broken into, and he had a lot to deal with. We decided to postpone our date.

Mike #80 was more into me and who I was. Mike #80 and I found out, right away, that both of us were born in Poland, which was not a plus for him, as I never wanted to date a Polish guy, like my father. But Mike #80 was raised in Bern, Switzrland, and this qualified him to be back in the game in my eyes. I always said that I would not date or marry a Polish guy, as this represented my father to me. To make things worse, he was a chemist, and my father was a chemist as well. Again, not a plus and really a minus. Taking all of this into account, I had no expectations from our first date. Mike #80 also worked long hours, and we could not find a time to meet, as he was working night shifts at the time he reached to me.

The only date that worked for both Mikes was July 4, 2015. Mike #79 closed his business early in the day for the holiday, and Mike #80 and I could meet in the morning, as I had a day off from work. I would have to have two dates on July Fourth, and it would not be the first time. I had no plans for the holiday and hadn't been invited to any fancy party that interested me. Most of my friends at the time were married and had young kids, so they would be spending the day with them. I was a free bird looking for a new nest and had no problem with it.

Both of them were a picnic date, which meant a potluck. We agreed on what each of us would bring "to the table," and I made sure to include wine for the afternoon date with Mike #79. It would be too early in the day to do the same with Mike #80. It also meant that I didn't have to dress up and spend too much time on makeup. I enjoyed the idea of no pressure and spending the day in nature.

Mike #80 was cute and looked much better than his nerdy picture. He was tall and handsome and very intelligent. Mike #80 brought a ton of fruit and some fancy cheese, and I admired his selection. I, on the other hand, brought a Polish spread that I was sure he would like, some crackers, and a plate of cut veggies with toothpicks to help us grab them. Of course, napkins, utensils, and paper plates were involved as well. I made sure that everything looked yummy and inviting. I liked doing things like that.

Mike #80 was very impressed from the selection to the presentation. I saw tears in his eyes when he saw the Polish spread of Pashted made from pork, and the toothpicks made his eyes open wide and a smile landed on his face for the rest of the date.

We had many common interests, and time flew by and after three hours, we were still there. I didn't know that Mike #80 had met me after a night shift at a major hospital in town. He hadn't slept in nearly twenty-four hours. But at no point did he say he was tired or had to leave. At one point, I had to apologize because I had to leave. Since I had another date later, I had to go home for a quick shower and to grab some more food. We ended the picnic with a mutual decision that we'd had fun and needed to meet again.

Mike #79 came to pick me from home. He had a known business in town, and I thought it was safe enough to give him my address. I also needed to carry a chair and a basket, so him coming and helping sounded like a good idea.

Mike #79 did not look like his picture and did not look like a biker. He was not in shape, had a beer belly, and his car had a trailer attached to it, that was usually used for motorcycles. That day it held all the picnic stuff we had brought. He had two Ducati folding chairs and was very proud of them. I had no idea what Ducati meant, so I had to Google it quickly without him noticing it, and then provided some wow comments from my side to make him happy.

It was a lovely picnic, good discussion, and great weather. Mike #79 brought strawberry vodka cocktails in Ducati takeout coffee tumblers, and I enjoyed every sip of it. He also brought some excellent cheese, and I brought the veggies—no toothpicks this time. We found a private spot on Green Lake Park and enjoyed watching the sun setting.

When Mike #79 drove me home, he helped me carry my stuff inside. He didn't wait too long and tried to kiss me in my kitchen. This was the point I asked him to leave, as I felt disgusted. He smelled like grease, and his belly was in his way as he grabbed me. I almost started to laugh. Mr. Ducati pulled himself away, not very gracefully, and assured me he would be in touch. I asked him to wait for a second and told him that I didn't see a match. To his credit, I have to say, he didn't argue and left wishing me all the best.

On the other hand, I was very curious to see what Mike #80's first text after our meeting would be. It had been five hours since we had ended our picnic, and I hadn't heard from him. I didn't know that the poor man had dropped dead on his bed after our date and slept for the next twelve hours. I got his text message at five the next morning, wishing me a happy Fourth of July and telling me what a great time he had had at the picnic the day before.

Mike #80 had already planned our next outing, which was another fun activity in the open air at the Polish festival at the Seattle Center. This was a big yearly festival, with which I was not familiar. I used to live on the eastside – about twenty-five miles from Seattle, so except driving to work every day, I tried not to drive to the city during the weekends. Since I moved to north Seattle, I discovered a new world of activities and plenty of places that I wanted to visit. Mike #80 had the same interests, and it looked like we could pair and enjoy them together. But the Polish festival was a week away, and I had a small gathering of friends at my place, a housewarming party, in two days. I invited Mike #80 to join us, as I knew he would enjoy the people and the conversations. I had an ex-Mike invited as well, as we had stopped dating but remained friends. I was sure that the two Mikes would be great together, both brilliant people and talkers.

On the day of the party, Mike #80 arrived almost an hour late, apologizing that he had just finished his shift — it was Saturday at three — and I assured him that all was fine, and he just needed to enjoy himself. To my surprise, Mike #80 was quiet and watched people from his place on the sofa for some time, until I sat next to him and asked him if he was okay. He assured me that all was fine and that he was just enjoying the discussions around him. He smiled at me when he said it, and his blue eyes looked sincere. I invited him to go out with me to the garden as I wanted to show him some new flowers I had planted. We were both avid gardeners, and Mike #80 had a lot of experience with growing different and weird plants. He was the first person I knew who had a ginger plant growing from scratch. I loved it.

When we went outside, we reached a corner where nobody could see us. I was cleaning that area and planting new flowers to bloom. Mike #80 caught me in the corner and kissed my lips very softly. He was 6' 2", and I was 5' 2". He had to bend down to get to me, and it was so cute! I blushed and felt my blood running fast. But I could not enjoy the moment for too long, as I had guests, and I heard somebody calling my name. It was the ex-Mike. He wondered where Mike #80 and I had disappeared. We came right back, smiling, and I kept the discussion going as if nothing had just happened when ex-Mike suddenly decided to ask — in a thunderous voice — why I was so red-faced. "Do you feel all right?" he asked.

I burst into a laugh and promised him I was doing great. Of course, everybody stopped everything and looked at me. I got redder. Mike #80 rescued the situation, by announcing that he was going to mix some drinks and asked who wanted what. This took the attention off me and onto him, which allowed me time to calm down and get my breathing back in order. I very much appreciated this gesture. It was brave and thoughtful of him. I felt he was a "keeper," and it had been a long time since I had felt like that.

Mike #80 had to leave early. He had another five-a.m. shift coming and needed to get back home in west Seattle and sleep. I appreciated his hard work and made him a plate to go with goodies that he could enjoy for breakfast and dinner. He was so happy. Mike #80 thanked me profusely and told me how much he appreciated it. So little sometimes takes us far. I received a beautiful bouquet of flowers on Monday at work, sent by Mike #80. Again, I knew he was a keeper.

At that point, I made a mistake in my dating documentation, and I was sure that he was #74, so I had a full week planned with dates in front of me and could not see Mike #80 for at least a week. He didn't complain and just said that he would be happy to see me whenever I was free. No pressure. A week later, I dropped all other dates and started seeing only Mike #80.

I'm going to let Mike #80 tell his story now, and it will all make sense.

From Paul L. Matusewicz AKA Mike #80:

I was fifty-four-years old, and my life, instead of slowing down, was speeding up like an amusement park roller coaster. My divorce was final, which meant I had to say goodbye to my comfortable west Seattle house, most of my savings, most of our mutual friends and, the hardest of all, daily life with my teenage daughters. From then on, I would only be able to see them on every other weekend. At work, I was put on nightshift—thank God just a temporary assignment—but, nevertheless, one that made me live in a permanent state of jet lag. Then my dad died, unexpectedly. We'd never had a good relationship, but he was still my only family in this country. I was flying to his funeral the same day I was closing on my condo. I still remember sitting on the tarmac ready to take off, my phone in my hand, desperately trying to sign off on the final papers while the stewardess was reciting all the laws I was breaking while refusing to put my phone down.

It was not a good time to see what was happening out there in terms of dating, but still, I was a guy who was interested in some fun in life. The news about my chances were pretty depressing: as far as Seattle was concerned. There were 136 guys for every one hundred women. Being an eternal optimist, I just saw a hundred single women waiting. Not a bad picture! I had my network of friends and a trusted dating site where I posted my profile. Now all I had to do was wait. And wait and wait... Okay, something there wasn't working out as I'd planned. Finally, I got a hit! A kind heart texted me: "Dude, your profile is really bad." Luckily, I thought fast and asked for advice. After some back and forth, this poor woman just gave up and wrote off my entire profile that I had just posted on my site. Without even reading it.

Dating, like looking for a job, was a number's game. Especially here in Seattle—remember 136:100. So, a guy had to contact about one hundred women to get a few hits. But with my new profile, I was at least getting hits, real hits. Dates at different coffee shops followed, and I was thinking more and more about buying some stock in those establishments. All the dates really added up and showed me there was potential for a business to grow. I had a lot of time to ponder new investments, because my dates were, well, weird. Some women had clear mental issues, some were just boring, some came bearing their own food and drinks. One exception was a nice painter of Russian origin, who is still my friend on Facebook.

Then came Sunday, June 28, a sweltering day and a day of an epic Seattle event, the Pride Parade! Every year I tried to be there with my friends. Also, there was this lady matched with me on the dating website. We had a ninety-four percent match, and we both "liked" each other, so I texted her. Back she wrote! While standing on the corner of Fourth Avenue and Bell Street. I asked if she was coming to the parade. "Been there, done that," was her answer.

A little disappointing answer. And yet a lot of texting followed:

Me: Where do you live?
Her: In north Seattle, just bought a condo.
Me: Ha, me, too! But in west Seattle.
Her: What are you doing?
Me: Hanging pictures, you?
Her: Guess what? Standing on a chair and hammering a hook in for a one big picture.
Me: How about now?
Her: Walking my dog.
Me: Me, too!

Come to think of it, in all those conversations, I never asked Renata (that was her name) what she looked like. Her only photo showed an ear. A cute one, with lovely earrings and a strand of blonde hair, but, nevertheless, just an ear! And so, it went for a few days, lots of texts about all possible subjects, including my favorite ones: Israel and stand-up shows. First time in my life I had met a woman who knew what I was talking about. We decided to meet on the Fourth of July, a Saturday, at Warren Magnusson Park located on the beautiful Lake Washington. The park had a beautiful off-leash area, which was perfect for both our dogs to run.

Fourth of July 2015 turned out to be one of the hottest days in Seattle's history, so we both decided to leave our beasts at home because it would be torture for them. We would just have a picnic in the park. Was I nervous? Not at all, it was so natural for me to meet this woman! Dressed in my comfortable shorts and flip flops, I waited in the parking lot. Renata was fashionably late, which I expected. And then this big car pulled into the lot, and a very short woman emerged carrying a lot of bags of food. We spread blankets on the lawn right next to the calm lake, comfortably in the shadows of trees. Renata spread out all the goodies.

Did I fall in love with her just then? I saw all these pates, little Polish cuts (I was born in Poland) she had prepared only for me. And every piece had a toothpick in them. Yes, I fell in love because of these toothpicks; they just represented that little extra this woman had done to make me comfortable. We still laugh about those toothpicks, but this little piece of wood did win my heart forever. We talked a lot, for a long time. How do I know? Well, we had to slide the blankets so many times, just to catch up with the moving shadows. Finally, it was getting late, and Renata had to go. Later I learned that she was running late for another date. Oh well, you can't have it all in the beginning.

Time went on, and we were meeting as often as we could in parks, beaches. After a few weeks, I took Renata out to a nice restaurant. I saw her at the door and I couldn't take my eyes off her when I saw her for the first time in an elegant dress. Until then, she had always worn shorts and sandals! I have known many women in my life, but never had I met anyone as beautiful as her.

Weeks turned into months. I traveled alone to Israel and met her family. We moved in together, shared good and bad moments. Even broke up for eighteen days, but

I never considered I would be with anyone but her. A year and a half from our date with toothpicks, we were married in a crazy Jewish-Indian ceremony—that's a long story. Renata still likes to surprise me, to this day, with toothpicks.

15 - TO DO OR NOT TO DO – INSTRUCTIONS FOR ONLINE DATING SITES

I learned many things during my experiences with the eighty Mikes about online dating sites. One of the most important things you should do before you even going online is to identify clearly, for yourself, what you want from the experience. Ask yourself the following questions:

- What stage in your life are you in right now?
- Are you looking just to have fun, and nothing more serious?
- Do you want to get married?
- Do you want to have kids? Are you ready to take care of somebody's else kids?
- Do you just want a companion when going out, watching a movie home, or on a cold winter day to beat the boredom?

Most of the online sites provide a "checkbox" for a majority of these questions, which helps you identify if the man who just wrote you is on the same page as you are.

Be true to yourself, first of all, and then consider the steps I learned along the way.

1. It all starts with your profile—the pictures you upload, the profile you write—this is what will attract the like-minded kind of men who you want to meet. There will always be exceptions, but this is an excellent way to filter unwanted men approaching you. Mention your intentions, what you are looking for, or discuss a particular skill you have that others might not have.
2. The more interactions you create, there are more chances to meet a man you will like.
3. Don't feel bad about saying no. If it all looks good, but you still have a bad gut feeling about it, don't hesitate to say, "thank you, but no thank you."
4. Free sites have all kinds of people on them. It is not entirely accurate that on the paid sites there are more "serious" people. Crazy people are everywhere.
5. Find something in common that you both like to do together. If you have a dog, mention it on your profile, and identify a brownie point for it. It provides encouragement to the other side, and also makes for a good opening line.

6. Look at his images on the account. Are they all from vacation pictures where you cannot see the person's face? You need at least one good image of his face and one good photograph of a full body. Ask when the photos were taken, or which one is the most recent.
7. Ask for a selfie from right now. This will eliminate not recognizing the person when you actually go on a date.
8. A big exception to #6 and #7 above—pictures say a lot but do not put all your weight on them. Some guys have horrible pictures, and you might just miss them. Some guys have great photos, but they are from five years ago.
9. Keep an open mind. You are going to bump into many guys who will not be nice. Do not let it take you down, and do not take it personally. Look at this as a journey and a way to get out of the house to meet new people and see new places. Have fun!
10. If you are using a site like OkCupid, answer as many questions as possible. Make sure to read the other person's answers as well, and not only the profile. You will find a lot of interesting information by looking at the responses provided. Sometimes the written reactions will not go well with the written profile. Identifying those gaps is essential.

11. Find out where they live, and if there is indeed a potential to meet and have a relationship, assuming you are not looking for a long distance one.
12. Ask what they do for a living. There are a lot of men who are not employed and will say that they are between jobs, they work a part-time job, or just remodeled a house and sold it. In reality, they have not been working for the past three years, the house was sold five years ago, and their part-time job means a contractor one-day job every couple of weeks. If you don't want to become their purse, this will help you figure out the situation very quickly. I remember a guy telling me that money was not necessary to him, and many great things in life are for free. On the fifth text message, I learned that he lived in a unit in his mother's house, and he was in his early fifties, had never married and had no kids. He blamed me for being a materialistic person because I mentioned the fact that it was weird, that a man in his age still lived at his mother's. "Okay," I answered, "let me stay materialistic, as I really enjoy being financially independent of my parents." He did not have any kind words to say.
13. Drinking and smoking habits. If your date drinks every day and smokes all day long, decide if this is something that will work for you. Make sure you are honest about your habits as well.

14. If kids are involved, ask about their ages, custody issues, and schedule. This will make clear if your date has time for you. The same about his work schedule.
15. If your future date brags about personal attributes in his profile (everybody said I'm so funny, all the women I dated said I'm a great dancer/good looking/the perfect gentleman/ a fantastic person), stop for a second and reread his profile. People who brag so much about themselves are usually not telling the truth. An excellent way to check is to read his answers/comments to different questions on a site like OkCupid.
16. Have a chat on the phone before going out on a date. Exception: If you are like me, and have an accent, you might not want to have a phone chat before a date. I find it hard to communicate on the phone with a stranger because of my accent.
17. The first date should be brief and in a neutral place, like a coffee shop. If the conversation goes well, you can always extend it. If it does not, it is easier to finish your coffee and say goodbye.
18. Movie or bowling is not a great idea for a first date. You want to have a discussion with your date, not compete with him over who is better in bowling or be quiet the whole time while watching a movie.

19. Take into account that ninety-nine men out of a hundred you will meet, will not be your cup of tea. Remember, you need only one. And, in the meantime, you might find some friends among all these people.
20. Do not chat forever. You want to see who you are talking to and decide if there is any chemistry in the air. If the other side is looking for a pen pal, it is not you, so continue in your quest.
21. You start chatting on the site, and it goes well. At this point take your chats off the site. Move to direct texting. If you see that the guy is still active on the online site, it is more than okay, and it is none of your business. You are on the site as well. I repeat: until you both decide to go "exclusive," the fact that he is still on the dating site, is none of your business. Also, do not mention it. You will sound like a crazy jealous woman and men detect it very fast.
22. There are men out there who are just like you — they are looking for a relationship, they are smart, real, and they have the same questions, and doubts as you do. Not everybody is crazy, but you will bump into some crazy ones, and it is part of the journey.
23. Make sure you are telling the truth about yourself, and your pictures are current (talk the talk, walk the walk.) Mention, in your profile, the month and year your photos were taken.

24. Do not share exposed body pictures, and then be surprised that you were approached only by the guys who are looking for casual sex.
25. Give it a chance. It might not happen on the first date, and it will take another couple of dates to identify if there is something in place that's worth the effort. Trust your gut, but also give it a chance.
26. If you think you are a queen and deserve the world, you might want to take a second look in the mirror and relax. You want to find the guy who will tell you that you are his queen, because he feels like it, and not because you think so. Shoving down his throat, from the beginning, is an excellent recipe for a "running away from you" contest.
27. Compromise, not because you don't want to be alone, but because you understand that nobody is perfect (besides you, of course.) Make sure that you are compromising on things that you can live with and accept in the daily life.
28. Say thank you for every message you get online, even if you do not like the pictures or the profile of the person who sent you the communication, assuming it was a friendly and polite message. If it was not a kind message, block the sender and report it to the site administrator.

29. When going on dates, make sure that a good friend/relative, knows that you are out there. Send them the date's name and phone number, and when and where you are meeting. If something goes wrong, you have a security blanket.
30. Ask to see your date's ID. You can learn the real name and age from it. If your future date refuses to share it with you, don't go on a date. Clarify that you are going to ask for it (explain why) before you go on a date and let them know that you are more than happy to share your ID with them as well. This one is a harsh one. Make sure you are using it wisely. The intention is not to insult anybody.
31. If you did choose to go on a date to a restaurant, don't order the most expensive item on the menu. If the guy is an old-school guy, he will insist on paying for it, and there is no reason he should feel that you are taking advantage of the situation.
32. Always—but always—offer to pay for your part in the date. If the guy insists that he is paying, at least you offered, and he made his decision.
33. If the guy tries to be physical on the first date, and you don't want to, tell him to stop, right away. If he does not, end the date on the spot, and do not hesitate for a second. The fact that you are staying and fighting with him makes him sometimes think that this is a game you are playing.

34. Everyday life brings with it a lot of challenges. You want a partner who you can count on, is equal to you, and does not put you down if you made a mistake. The same goes for you.
35. If you don't feel that this is the right person, just stop and finish the date. Say thank you, and do not continue the chat/text/date. In case you went for coffee or a short date, be polite and stay until the end.
36. Imagination is often better than reality. This is how we all fill the gaps, in over-optimistic terms. Be careful there, it might be very disappointing (He likes music, so for sure we can be together. But he likes hard rock, you like classical music.)
37. How do you make a meaningful discussion on an online dating site? Do not make it an interview and review it as a resume. Talk about yourself, what you like, hobbies you enjoy that can include a significant other such as dancing, hiking, cooking, traveling.
38. What are you trying to get out of a date? You want to see a person's behavior in a real world, right? Go to a place where there will be interactions with others and be yourself. He is watching you as well. An empty room will not work, so get to know your date.

39. Playing hard to get or cognitive dissonance. You worked hard to get to the date and are doing your best. But it is not a guy who you usually pursue, so tell yourself that this was not a waste of time. Learn how to move on quickly.
40. Women have the power in the online dating world. Men might send one hundred messages and get two messages in return. Initiate on your side when you see a profile you like, and don't let it be only "luck" that the right guy will see your profile.
41. Some men apparently did not read your profile, and just send you a "Hi" message, which is not what you would like to see. Remember, there is a person on the other side, and maybe it's not his best day, or he's been through a lot and feels a little down with all the no replies until yours. Give them a break. Look at his profile; he did choose to send you a message, maybe there is a good reason for that.
42. Appreciate that somebody made an effort and came to meet you. He might live far away, he might have had a hard day at work, but he is there. Don't take it for granted.

43. Expectation and investment - it is easy to flip to the next picture, or not put an effort if you think you can do better, with few more profiles. Think about renting on a daily basis, where you and your landlord can decide every day whether you continue to rent or not. How much effort will you put in this place? Decorate it? Love it?
44. Opportunity and investments. From a scale of 1 to 10, this guy is 8.5. Will you invest the time to know him better? Will you take the time to learn more about him, or will you decide to continue looking? It might take you another three years and no results. Three years from now, you will not be the same person anymore.
45. When you are in love and infatuated, you do not see things. Ask a good friend—or your mother could be the right person to ask if she is still around and trust her opinion. You want your friends to give their honest judgment, if they see a fit between you and him. Make sure it's a fit for you. He might be fantastic for them and not for you. The same thing goes for you, when a friend is asking for your opinion—be true and give it to them. Too many people are politically correct even with their family and close friends.
46. Banana or canoeing whitewater test – when I slip on a banana, it is the fault of the person who threw it. When somebody else slips on a banana, it is their fault for not looking where they are going. In a canoe trip, you are facing situations that you

cannot predict. How does your date handle it? Does he blame you, encourage you, or shout at you?

47. "The grass is always greener, and the next profile will be better." This declaration is not true. Take the time to read and listen, don't just swipe right and left, if you want to meet a person that interests you.

48. Profiles and pictures are like looking at a menu, when the dishes are described with a list of nutrition, calories, and ingredients. A menu like this will not make you want to eat. Same with online dating profiles. A list of things and few pictures do not have any flavor. Find something that you like to do and share it with your date or on your profile. For me, it was traveling and different cultures. It was my priority to find somebody who was curious about the world, loved to learn, and meet new people. If somebody was a homebody who liked to watch TV, it would not have worked for either of us.

49. The end result matters a great deal. What could be the end result of your dating experience? Take a moment and think about it. But don't forget the journey and enjoy it.

50. Stay positive. A bad date is not the end of the world. Think about the end results. What are the positive results that will come out of it? How much will your life resemble the one you want with that person?

THANK YOU

Hi, stranger,

    I hope you enjoyed *Around Seattle in 80 Dates -- An Online Dating Journey,* and by the end of it you felt that something new had entered your life, and we weren't strangers anymore.

    I would love to hear your thoughts in a review on the retail site where you purchased it. Reviews are very helpful to all authors. Also, tell your friends about it. Word of mouth is an author's best friend and much appreciated. Again, thank you.

Cheers, Renata

RESOURCES

On Dating & Relationships, Dr. Dan Ariely, Talks at Google - http://bit.ly/1SAeVwT

100 dates in 100 days: Nailing the Man of Your Dreams Without Getting Screwed. Neha Gupta - http://amzn.to/2EiJrrX

How I Hacked Online Dating, Amy Webb - http://bit.ly/2nB2Jjl

The Secret to Desire in a Long-Term Relationship, Ester Perel - http://bit.ly/2HavUEI

Modern Romance: An Investigation, Aziz Ansari and Eric Klinenberg - http://bit.ly/2H8XkuN

ABOUT THE AUTHOR

After thirty-two years in one relationship, Renata Lubinsky divorced her husband and started a journey that she crafted on a daily basis, by using online dating sites.

Renata's massive experience in the online dating world and her love for the unexpected provided her with mesmerizing material that will make you laugh out loud in some stories, and in others, make you cry.

Renata uses her witty and sensitive voice to describe the world from the perspective of a single, almost fifty-year-old woman starting the second chapter of her life.

In the past few years, Renata has taken her stories on stage and performed in different stand-up events around Seattle. She has won first place in local stand-up competitions and participated in various storytelling shows.

Made in the USA
Middletown, DE
31 March 2018